everyday

muffins & bakes

LOVE FOOD™

This edition published in 2010
LOVE FOOD is an imprint of Parragon Books Ltd

Parragon
Queen Street House
4 Queen Street
Bath BA1 1HE, UK

ISBN: 978-1-4054-8679-8

Printed in China

Designed by Terry Jeavons & Company

Notes for the Reader
This book uses both metric and imperial measurements. Follow the same units of measurement throughout; do not mix metric and imperial. All spoon measurements are level: teaspoons are assumed to be 5 ml, and tablespoons are assumed to be 15 ml. Unless otherwise stated, milk is assumed to be full fat, eggs and individual vegetables are medium, and pepper is freshly ground black pepper.

The times given are an approximate guide only. Preparation times differ according to the techniques used by different people and the cooking times may also vary from those given. Optional ingredients, variations or serving suggestions have not been included in the calculations.

Recipes using raw or very lightly cooked eggs should be avoided by infants, the elderly, pregnant women, convalescents and anyone suffering from an illness. Pregnant and breastfeeding women are advised to avoid eating peanuts and peanut products. Sufferers from nut allergies should be aware that some of the ready-made ingredients used in the recipes in this book may contain nuts. Always check the packaging before use.

everyday muffins & bakes

introduction

Muffins, cupcakes, biscuits, bars and traybakes are without doubt the most versatile sweet treat you can make. While a large cake looks impressive, especially if it is beautifully decorated with frosting, it can really only be eaten from a plate, probably with a dessert fork. An individual cake, on the other hand, will travel, making it ideal for putting in a lunch box, taking on a picnic, even just taken into the garden for a mid-morning or afternoon snack.

This really does not make an individual cake any less special, however, because – as you will discover when you start baking – these one-person treasures are packed full of the most sumptuous

ingredients, from fresh or dried fruits to chocolate and nuts. We've even included an equally delicious 'healthy options' section so that you won't miss out if you are keeping an eye on your intake of fats and sugar.

Of course, practicality isn't always the first consideration, and there are plenty of ideas for making sweet treats with more than a hint of indulgence! Frostings, decorations and flavourings such as liqueurs turn a cake into a celebration, and we've included a section especially for those special occasions in life. The romantic at heart can chart a whole marriage in muffins, cupcakes and biscuits, from Valentine's day and the wedding day to the baby shower and the silver and golden wedding anniversaries, with all the birthday parties and other festive occasions along the way!

Baking is a great way to pass the time on a rainy day, and these recipes are ideal for children to help with – muffins and cupcakes need very little mixing, and take only minutes to cook. Children will love helping to decorate gingerbread people, party cookies, fairy cakes, and cupcakes to celebrate Christmas, Easter, and Halloween – and they will certainly love to eat them, too!

fruit & nut

Children can be notoriously difficult when it comes to eating fruit and vegetables, but they are soon converted when they try Apple and Cinnamon Muffins, warm from the oven and sprinkled with crushed sugar lumps, spicy Carrot and Orange Cupcakes with Mascarpone Frosting or Summer Fruit Tartlets, a delicious nutty pastry crust with currants and berries nestling on a cream cheese filling.

Muffins are the ideal lunch box treat because they are relatively low in fat and sugar, and – as long as your child doesn't have a nut allergy – you can add in some useful protein. Try Banana Pecan Muffins, or Nectarine and Banana.

If you are having friends round for morning coffee or afternoon tea and want to serve something a little more sophisticated, you will really be spoilt for choice. Try Fig and Almond Muffins or Fudge Nut Muffins – both heavenly! Warm Strawberry Cupcakes Baked in a Teacup will be a wonderful talking point and solve the mystery as to why cupcakes are so called!

If you don't mind getting sticky fingers, the Frosted Peanut Butter Cupcakes are gorgeous, and Baklava, a Middle Eastern specialty of crisp filo pastry packed with a spicy nut mixture and topped with orange-flavour syrup, is irresistibly messy to eat!

apple & cinnamon muffins

ingredients

MAKES 6

- 85 g/3 oz plain wholewheat flour
- 70 g/2½ oz plain white flour
- 1½ tsp baking powder
- pinch of salt
- 1 tsp ground cinnamon
- 40 g/1½ oz golden caster sugar
- 2 small eating apples, peeled, cored and finely chopped
- 125 ml/4 fl oz milk
- 1 egg, beaten
- 4 tbsp butter, melted

topping

- 12 brown sugar lumps, roughly crushed
- ½ tsp ground cinnamon

method

1 Place 6 muffin paper cases in a muffin pan.

2 Sift both flours, baking powder, salt and cinnamon together into a large bowl and stir in the sugar and chopped apples. Place the milk, egg and butter in a separate bowl and mix. Add the wet ingredients to the dry ingredients and gently stir until just combined.

3 Divide the mixture evenly between the paper cases. To make the topping, mix the crushed sugar lumps and cinnamon together and sprinkle over the muffins. Bake in a preheated oven, 200°C/400°F, for 20–25 minutes or until risen and golden. Remove the muffins from the oven and serve warm or place them on a wire rack to cool.

cranberry & cheese muffins

ingredients

MAKES 18

butter, for greasing
225 g/8 oz plain flour
2 tsp baking powder
1/2 tsp salt
55 g/2 oz caster sugar
4 tbsp butter, melted
2 large eggs, lightly beaten
175 ml/6 fl oz milk
115 g/4 oz fresh cranberries
25 g/1 oz freshly grated Parmesan cheese

method

1 Lightly grease 2 x 9-cup muffin pans with butter.

2 Sift the flour, baking powder and salt into a mixing bowl. Stir in the caster sugar.

3 In a separate bowl, combine the butter, beaten eggs and milk, then pour into the bowl of dry ingredients. Mix lightly together until all of the ingredients are evenly combined, then stir in the fresh cranberries.

4 Divide the mixture evenly between the prepared 18 cups in the muffin pans. Sprinkle the grated Parmesan cheese over the top. Transfer to a preheated oven, 200°C/400°F, and bake for 20 minutes or until the muffins are well risen and a golden brown colour.

5 Remove the muffins from the oven and let them cool slightly in the pans. Place the muffins on a wire rack and cool completely.

dried cherry cheesecake muffins

ingredients

MAKES 12

150 g/5 1/2 oz butter, plus extra for greasing
200 g/7 oz cream cheese
150 g/5 1/2 oz caster sugar
3 large eggs, lightly beaten
300 g/10 1/2 oz self-raising flour
100 g/3 1/2 oz dried cherries, chopped
icing sugar, for dusting

method

1 Grease a deep 12-cup muffin pan.

2 Melt the butter and cool slightly. In a large bowl, whisk the cream cheese and sugar together, add the eggs one at a time until well combined and then stir in the melted butter.

3 Mix the flour and cherries in a bowl, then stir gently into the mixture. Spoon into the prepared muffin pan, filling each hole to about two-thirds full, and bake in a preheated oven, 180°C/350°F, for 12–15 minutes or until golden brown. Remove from the oven and cool on a wire rack. Eat warm or cold, dusted lightly with icing sugar.

banana pecan muffins

ingredients

MAKES 8

150 g/5$^{1}/_{2}$ oz plain flour
1$^{1}/_{2}$ tsp baking powder
pinch of salt
70 g/2$^{1}/_{2}$ oz golden caster sugar
115 g/4 oz shelled pecan nuts, roughly chopped
2 large ripe bananas, mashed
5 tbsp milk
2 tbsp butter, melted
1 large egg, beaten
$^{1}/_{2}$ tsp vanilla essence

method

1 Place 8 muffin paper cases in a muffin pan. Sift the flour, baking powder and salt into a bowl, add the sugar and pecan nuts and stir to combine.

2 Place the mashed bananas, milk, butter, egg and vanilla essence in a separate bowl and mix together. Add the wet ingredients to the dry ingredients and gently stir until just combined.

3 Divide the mixture evenly between the paper cases and bake in a preheated oven, 190°C/375°F, for 20–25 minutes or until risen and golden. Remove the muffins from the oven and place them on a wire rack to cool.

nectarine & banana muffins

ingredients

SERVES 12

- 75 ml/2$^1/_2$ fl oz sunflower or peanut oil, plus extra for oiling (if using)
- 250 g/9 oz plain flour
- 1 tsp bicarbonate of soda
- $^1/_4$ tsp salt
- $^1/_4$ tsp allspice
- 100 g/3$^1/_2$ oz caster sugar
- 55 g/2 oz shelled almonds, chopped
- 175 g/6 oz ripe nectarine, peeled and chopped
- 1 ripe banana, sliced
- 2 large eggs
- 75 ml/2$^1/_2$ fl oz thick natural or banana-flavoured yogurt
- 1 tsp almond essence

method

1 Oil a 12-cup muffin pan with sunflower oil, or line it with 12 muffin paper cases. Sift the flour, bicarbonate of soda, salt and allspice into a mixing bowl. Add the caster sugar and chopped almonds and stir together.

2 In a separate large bowl, mash the nectarine and banana together, then stir in the eggs, remaining sunflower oil, yogurt and almond essence. Add the mashed fruit mixture to the flour mixture and then gently stir together until just combined. Do not overstir the mixture – it is fine for it to be a little lumpy.

3 Divide the muffin mixture evenly between the 12 cups in the muffin pan or the paper cases (they should be about two-thirds full). Transfer to a preheated oven, 200°C/400°F, and bake for 20 minutes or until risen and golden. Serve warm from the oven, or place them on a wire rack to cool.

tropical coconut muffins

ingredients

MAKES 12

- 1 tbsp sunflower or peanut oil, for oiling (if using)
- 250 g/9 oz plain flour
- 1 tsp baking powder
- 1 tsp bicarbonate of soda
- 1/2 tsp allspice
- 115 g/4 oz butter
- 225 g/8 oz brown sugar
- 2 large eggs, beaten
- 2 tbsp thick natural, banana or pineapple-flavoured yogurt
- 1 tbsp rum
- 1 ripe banana, sliced
- 75 g/2 3/4 oz canned pineapple rings, drained and chopped
- 55 g/2 oz dessicated coconut

coconut topping

- 4 tbsp raw sugar
- 1 tsp allspice
- 25 g/1 oz dessicated coconut

method

1 Oil a 12-cup muffin pan with sunflower oil or line it with 12 muffin paper cases. Sift the flour, baking powder, bicarbonate of soda and allspice into a mixing bowl.

2 In a separate large bowl, cream together the butter and brown sugar, then stir in the eggs, yogurt and rum. Add the banana, pineapple and dessicated coconut and mix together gently. Add the pineapple mixture to the flour mixture and then gently stir together until just combined. Do not overstir the mixture – it is fine for it to be a little lumpy.

3 Divide the muffin mixture evenly between the 12 cups in the muffin pan or the paper cases (they should be about two-thirds full). To make the topping, mix the raw sugar and allspice together and sprinkle over the muffins. Sprinkle over the dessicated coconut, then transfer to a preheated oven, 200°C/400°F. Bake for 20 minutes or until risen and golden. Remove the muffins from the oven and serve warm, or place them on a wire rack to cool.

fig & almond muffins

ingredients

MAKES 12

- 2 tbsp sunflower or peanut oil, plus extra for oiling (if using)
- 250 g/9 oz plain flour
- 1 tsp bicarbonate of soda
- 1/2 tsp salt
- 225 g/8 oz raw sugar
- 85 g/3 oz dried figs, chopped
- 115 g/4 oz almonds, chopped
- 200 ml/7 fl oz water
- 1 tsp almond essence
- 2 tbsp chopped almonds, to decorate

method

1 Oil a 12-cup muffin pan with sunflower oil, or line it with 12 muffin paper cases. Sift the flour, bicarbonate of soda and salt into a mixing bowl. Add the raw sugar and stir together.

2 In a separate bowl, mix the figs, almonds and remaining sunflower oil together. Then stir in the water and almond essence. Add the fruit and nut mixture to the flour mixture and gently stir together. Do not overstir – it is fine for it to be a little lumpy.

3 Divide the muffin mixture evenly between the 12 cups in the muffin pan or the paper cases (they should be about two-thirds full), then sprinkle over the remaining chopped almonds to decorate. Transfer to a preheated oven, 190°C/375°F, and bake for 25 minutes or until risen and golden.

4 Remove the muffins from the oven and serve warm, or place them on a wire rack to cool.

fudge nut muffins

ingredients

MAKES 12

250 g/9 oz plain flour
4 tsp baking powder
85 g/3 oz caster sugar
6 tbsp crunchy peanut butter
1 large egg, beaten
4 tbsp butter, melted
175 ml/6 fl oz milk
150 g/5½ oz vanilla fudge, cut into small pieces
3 tbsp roughly chopped unsalted peanuts

method

1 Line a 12-cup muffin pan with double muffin paper cases. Sift the flour and baking powder into a bowl. Stir in the caster sugar. Add the peanut butter and stir until the mixture resembles breadcrumbs.

2 Place the egg, butter and milk in a separate bowl and beat until blended, then stir into the dry ingredients until just blended. Lightly stir in the fudge pieces. Divide the mixture evenly between the muffin paper cases.

3 Sprinkle the chopped peanuts on top and bake in a preheated oven, 200°C/400°F, for 20–25 minutes or until well risen and firm to the touch. Remove the muffins from the oven and cool for 2 minutes, then place them on a wire rack to cool completely.

apple streusel cupcakes

ingredients

MAKES 14

1/2 tsp bicarbonate of soda
280-g/10-oz jar apple sauce
4 tbsp butter, softened, or soft margarine
85 g/3 oz raw brown sugar
1 large egg, lightly beaten
175 g/6 oz self-raising flour
1/2 tsp ground cinnamon
1/2 tsp freshly ground nutmeg

topping

50 g/1 3/4 oz plain flour
50 g/1 3/4 oz raw brown sugar
1/4 tsp ground cinnamon
1/4 tsp freshly grated nutmeg
2 1/2 tbsp butter

method

1 Put 14 paper baking cases in a muffin pan, or place 14 double-layer paper cases on a baking sheet.

2 First make the topping. Put the flour, sugar, cinnamon and nutmeg in a bowl or in the bowl of a food processor. Cut the butter into small pieces, then either rub it in by hand or blend in the processor until the mixture resembles fine breadcrumbs. Set aside while you make the cakes.

3 To make the cupcakes, add the bicarbonate of soda to the jar of apple sauce and stir until dissolved. Put the butter and sugar in a bowl and beat together until light and fluffy. Gradually beat in the egg. Sift in the flour, cinnamon and nutmeg and, using a large metal spoon, fold into the mixture, alternating with the apple sauce.

4 Spoon the mixture into the paper cases. Sprinkle a little topping over each cupcake to cover the tops and press down gently.

5 Bake the cupcakes in a preheated oven, 180°C/350°F, for 20 minutes or until well risen and golden brown. Leave the cakes for 2–3 minutes before serving warm or transfer to a wire rack to cool.

carrot & orange cupcakes with mascarpone frosting

ingredients

MAKES 12

8 tbsp butter, softened, or soft margarine
115 g/4 oz brown sugar
juice and finely grated rind of 1 small orange
2 large eggs, lightly beaten
175 g/6 oz carrots, grated
25 g/1 oz walnut pieces, roughly chopped
125 g/4½ oz plain flour
1 tsp ground mixed spice
1½ tsp baking powder

frosting

280 g/10 oz Mascarpone cheese
4 tbsp icing sugar
grated rind of 1 large orange

method

1 Put 12 muffin paper cases in a muffin pan.

2 Put the butter, sugar and orange rind in a bowl and beat together until light and fluffy. Gradually add the eggs, beating well after each addition. Squeeze any excess liquid from the carrots and add to the mixture with the walnuts and orange juice. Stir into the mixture until well mixed. Sift in the flour, mixed spice and baking powder and then, using a metal spoon, fold into the mixture. Spoon the mixture into the paper cases.

3 Bake the cupcakes in a preheated oven, 180°C/350°F, for 25 minutes or until well risen, firm to the touch and golden brown. Transfer to a wire rack to cool.

4 To make the frosting, put the Mascarpone cheese, icing sugar and orange rind in a large bowl and beat together until well mixed.

5 When the cupcakes are cold, spread a little frosting on top of each, swirling it with a round-bladed knife. Store the cupcakes in the refrigerator until ready to serve.

shredded orange cupcakes

ingredients

MAKES 12

6 tbsp butter, softened, or soft margarine
85 g/3 oz caster sugar
1 large egg, lightly beaten
85 g/3 oz self-raising flour
25 g/1 oz ground almonds
grated rind and juice of 1 small orange

orange topping

1 orange
55 g/2 oz caster sugar
15 g/½ oz toasted flaked almonds

method

1 Put 12 paper baking cases in a muffin pan, or put 12 double-layer paper cases on a baking sheet.

2 Put the butter and sugar in a bowl and beat together until light and fluffy. Gradually beat in the egg. Add the flour, ground almonds and orange rind and, using a large metal spoon, fold into the mixture. Fold in the orange juice. Spoon the mixture into the paper cases.

3 Bake the cupcakes in a preheated oven, 180°C/350°F, for 20–25 minutes or until well risen and golden brown.

4 Meanwhile, make the topping. Using a citrus zester, pare the rind from the orange, then squeeze the juice. Put the rind, juice and sugar in a saucepan and heat gently, stirring, until the sugar has dissolved, then simmer for 5 minutes.

5 When the cupcakes have cooked, prick them all over with a skewer. Spoon a little warm syrup and rind over each cupcake, then sprinkle the flaked almonds on top. Transfer to a wire rack to cool.

cranberry cupcakes

ingredients

MAKES 14

- $5^1/_2$ tbsp butter, softened, or soft margarine
- 100 g/$3^1/_2$ oz caster sugar
- 1 large egg
- 2 tbsp milk
- 100 g/$3^1/_2$ oz self-raising flour
- 1 tsp baking powder
- 75 g/$2^3/_4$ oz cranberries, frozen

method

1 Put 14 paper baking cases in a muffin pan, or place 14 double-layer paper cases on a baking sheet.

2 Put the butter and sugar in a bowl and beat together until light and fluffy. Gradually beat in the egg, then stir in the milk. Sift in the flour and baking powder and, using a large metal spoon, fold them into the mixture. Gently fold in the frozen cranberries. Spoon the mixture into the paper cases.

3 Bake the cupcakes in a preheated oven, 180°C/350°F, for 15–20 minutes or until well risen and golden brown. Transfer to a wire rack to cool.

coconut cherry cupcakes

ingredients

MAKES 12

8 tbsp butter, softened, or soft margarine
115 g/4 oz caster sugar
2 tbsp milk
2 eggs, lightly beaten
85 g/3 oz self-raising flour
1/2 tsp baking powder
85 g/3 oz dessicated coconut
115 g/4 oz glacé cherries, quartered
12 whole glacé, maraschino or fresh cherries, to decorate

frosting

4 tbsp butter, softened
115 g/4 oz icing sugar
1 tbsp milk

method

1 Put 12 paper baking cases in a muffin pan, or place 12 double-layer paper cases on a baking sheet.

2 Put the butter and sugar in a bowl and beat together until light and fluffy. Stir in the milk. Gradually add the eggs, beating well after each addition. Sift in the flour and baking powder and fold them in with the coconut. Gently fold in most of the quartered cherries, then spoon the mixture into the paper cases and sprinkle the remaining quartered cherries over the top.

3 Bake the cupcakes in a preheated oven, 180°C/350°F, for 20–25 minutes or until well risen, golden brown and firm to the touch. Transfer to a wire rack to cool.

4 To make the buttercream frosting, put the butter in a bowl and beat until fluffy. Sift in the icing sugar and beat together until well mixed, gradually beating in the milk.

5 To decorate the cupcakes, using a piping bag fitted with a large star tip, pipe a little frosting on top of each cupcake, then add a glacé, maraschino or fresh cherry to decorate.

tropical pineapple cupcakes with citrus cream frosting

ingredients

MAKES 12

2 slices of canned pineapple in natural juice
6 tbsp butter, softened, or soft margarine
85 g/3 oz caster sugar
1 large egg, lightly beaten
85 g/3 oz self-raising flour
1 tbsp juice from the canned pineapple

frosting

2 tbsp butter, softened
100 g/3½ oz soft cream cheese
grated rind of 1 lemon or lime
100 g/3½ oz icing sugar
1 tsp lemon juice or lime juice

method

1 Put 12 paper baking cases in a muffin pan, or place 12 double-layer paper cases on a baking sheet.

2 Finely chop the pineapple slices. Put the butter and sugar in a bowl and beat together until light and fluffy. Gradually beat in the egg. Add the flour and, using a large metal spoon, fold into the mixture. Fold in the chopped pineapple and the pineapple juice. Spoon the mixture into the paper cases.

3 Bake the cupcakes in a preheated oven, 180°C/350°F, for 20 minutes or until well risen and golden brown. Transfer to a wire rack to cool.

4 To make the frosting, put the butter and cream cheese in a large bowl and, using an electric hand whisk, beat together until smooth. Add the rind from the lemon or lime. Sift the icing sugar into the mixture, then beat together until well mixed. Gradually beat in the juice from the lemon or lime, adding enough to form a spreading consistency.

5 When the cupcakes are cold, spread a little frosting on top of each cake, or fill a piping bag fitted with a large star tip and pipe the frosting on top. Store the cupcakes in the refrigerator until ready to serve.

warm strawberry cupcakes baked in a teacup

ingredients

MAKES 6

8 tbsp butter, softened, plus extra for greasing
4 tbsp strawberry conserve
115 g/4 oz caster sugar
2 eggs, lightly beaten
1 tsp vanilla essence
115 g/4 oz self-raising flour
450 g/1 lb small whole fresh strawberries
icing sugar, for dusting

method

1 Grease 6 heavy, round teacups with butter. Spoon 2 teaspoons of the strawberry conserve in the bottom of each teacup.

2 Put the butter and sugar in a bowl and beat together until light and fluffy. Gradually add the eggs, beating well after each addition, then add the vanilla essence. Sift in the flour and, using a large metal spoon, fold it into the mixture. Spoon the mixture into the teacups.

3 Stand the cups in a roasting tin, then pour in enough hot water to come one-third of the way up the sides of the cups. Bake the cupcakes in a preheated oven, 180°C/350°F, for 40 minutes or until well risen and golden brown and a skewer inserted in the centre comes out clean. If over-browning, cover the cupcakes with a sheet of foil. Leave the cupcakes to cool for 2–3 minutes, then carefully lift the cups from the tin and place them on saucers.

4 Place a few whole strawberries on each cake, then dust them with a little sifted icing sugar. Serve warm with the remaining strawberries.

moist walnut cupcakes

ingredients

MAKES 12

85 g/3 oz walnuts
4 tbsp butter, softened
100 g/3½ oz caster sugar
grated rind of ½ lemon
70 g/2½ oz self-raising flour
2 eggs
12 walnut halves, to decorate

frosting

4 tbsp butter, softened
85 g/3 oz icing sugar
grated rind of ½ lemon
1 tsp lemon juice

method

1 Put 12 paper baking cases in a muffin pan, or place 12 double-layer paper cases on a baking sheet.

2 Put the walnuts in a food processor and, using a pulsating action, blend until finely ground, being careful not to overgrind, which will turn them to oil. Add the butter, cut into small pieces, along with the sugar, lemon rind, flour and eggs, then blend until evenly mixed. Spoon the mixture into the paper cases.

3 Bake the cupcakes in a preheated oven, 190°C/375°F, for 20 minutes or until well risen and golden brown. Transfer to a wire rack to cool.

4 To make the frosting, put the butter in a bowl and beat until fluffy. Sift in the icing sugar, add the lemon rind and juice, and mix well.

5 When the cupcakes are cold, spread a little frosting on top of each cupcake and top with a walnut half to decorate.

banana & pecan cupcakes

ingredients

MAKES 24

225 g/8 oz plain flour
1¼ tsp baking powder
¼ tsp bicarbonate of soda
2 ripe bananas
8 tbsp butter, softened, or soft margarine
115 g/4 oz caster sugar
½ tsp vanilla essence
2 eggs, lightly beaten
4 tbsp sour cream
55 g/2 oz pecan nuts, roughly chopped

topping

8 tbsp butter, softened
115 g/4 oz icing sugar
25 g/1 oz pecan nuts, finely chopped

method

1 Put 24 paper baking cases in 2 muffin pans, or place 24 double-layer paper cases on a baking sheet.

2 Sift together the flour, baking powder and bicarbonate of soda. Peel the bananas, put them in a bowl and mash with a fork.

3 Put the butter, sugar and vanilla in a bowl and beat together until light and fluffy. Gradually add the eggs, beating well after each addition. Stir in the mashed bananas and sour cream. Using a metal spoon, fold in the sifted flour mixture and chopped nuts, then spoon the mixture into the paper cases.

4 Bake the cupcakes in a preheated oven, 190°C/375°F, for 20 minutes or until well risen and golden brown. Transfer to a wire rack to cool.

5 To make the topping, beat the butter in a bowl until fluffy. Sift in the icing sugar and mix together well. Spread a little frosting on top of each cupcake and sprinkle with the finely chopped pecan nuts before serving.

frosted peanut butter cupcakes

ingredients

MAKES 16

4 tbsp butter, softened, or soft margarine
225 g/8 oz brown sugar
115 g/4 oz crunchy peanut butter
2 eggs, lightly beaten
1 tsp vanilla essence
225 g/8 oz plain flour
2 tsp baking powder
100 ml/3½ fl oz milk

frosting

200 g/7 oz full-fat soft cream cheese
2 tbsp butter, softened
225 g/8 oz icing sugar

method

1 Put 16 muffin paper cases in a muffin pan.

2 Put the butter, sugar and peanut butter in a bowl and beat together for 1–2 minutes, or until well mixed. Gradually add the eggs, beating well after each addition, then add the vanilla essence. Sift in the flour and baking powder and then, using a metal spoon, fold them into the mixture, alternating with the milk. Spoon the mixture into the paper cases.

3 Bake the cupcakes in a preheated oven, 180°C/350°F, for 25 minutes or until well risen and golden brown. Transfer to a wire rack to cool.

4 To make the frosting, put the cream cheese and butter in a large bowl and, using an electric hand whisk, beat together until smooth. Sift the icing sugar into the mixture, then beat together until well mixed.

5 When the cupcakes are cold, spread a little frosting on top of each cupcake, swirling it with a round-bladed knife. Store the cupcakes in the refrigerator until ready to serve.

maple pecan tarts

ingredients

MAKES 12

pastry

150 g/5½ oz plain flour, plus extra for dusting
6 tbsp butter
55 g/2 oz golden caster sugar
2 egg yolks

filling

2 tbsp maple syrup
150 ml/5 fl oz double cream
115 g/4 oz golden caster sugar
pinch of cream of tartar
6 tbsp water
175 g/6 oz pecan nuts
12 pecan nut halves, to decorate

method

1 Sift the flour into a large bowl, then cut the butter into pieces and rub it into the flour using your fingertips until the mixture resembles breadcrumbs. Stir in the sugar, then stir in the egg yolks to make a smooth dough. Wrap in clingfilm and chill in the refrigerator for 30 minutes.

2 On a floured work surface, roll out the pastry thinly, cut out circles and use to line 12 tartlet tins. Prick the bottoms and press a piece of foil into each tart case. Bake in a preheated oven, 200°C/400°F, for 10–15 minutes or until light golden. Remove the foil and bake for a further 2–3 minutes. Cool on a wire rack.

3 To make the filling, mix together half the maple syrup and half the cream in a bowl. Place the sugar, cream of tartar and water in a saucepan over low heat and stir until the sugar dissolves. Bring to the boil and boil until light golden. Remove from the heat and stir in the maple syrup and cream mixture.

4 Return to the heat and cook to the 'soft ball' stage (116°C/240°F), when a little of the mixture forms a soft ball when dropped into cold water. Stir in the remaining cream and stand until warm. Brush the remaining maple syrup over the edges of the tarts. Place the pecans in the pastry cases, spoon in the toffee and top with a nut half. Cool before serving.

baklava

ingredients

MAKES 20 PIECES

115 g/4 oz blanched almonds
115 g/4 oz walnuts
115 g/4 oz shelled pistachios
55 g/2 oz brown sugar
1 tsp ground cinnamon
1/2 tsp freshly grated nutmeg
55 g/2 oz butter, melted, plus extra for greasing
12 sheets ready-made filo pastry, about 30 x 18 cm/12 x 7 inches

syrup

225 g/8 oz granulated sugar
150 ml/5 fl oz water
1 tbsp lemon juice
1 tbsp orange-flower water

method

1 To make the syrup, place the sugar, water and lemon juice in a saucepan over low heat and stir until the sugar has completely dissolved, then boil gently for 5 minutes, until the mixture takes on a syrupy consistency. Add the orange-flower water and boil for a further 2 minutes. Cool completely.

2 Place one-third of all the nuts in a food processor and process until finely chopped. Roughly chop the remainder. Place all the chopped nuts in a bowl with the sugar, cinnamon and nutmeg and mix together.

3 Grease a baking pan that is roughly the same size as, or slightly smaller than, the sheets of pastry. Brush 1 sheet of pastry with butter and place on the bottom of the baking pan. Repeat with 3 more sheets. Spread one-third of the nut mixture over the pastry. Top with 2 more layers of buttered pastry, then another third of the nut mixture. Top with 2 more buttered filo sheets, then the remaining nuts. Finally top with 4 sheets of buttered filo.

4 Cut the top layer of pastry into diamonds and bake in a preheated oven, 180°C/350°F, for 30–40 minutes or until crisp and golden. Remove from the oven, pour the syrup over the top and cool. When cold, trim the edges and cut into diamond shapes.

summer fruit tartlets

ingredients

MAKES 12

pastry

200 g/7 oz plain flour, plus extra for dusting
85 g/3 oz icing sugar
55 g/2 oz ground almonds
115 g/4 oz butter
1 egg yolk
1 tbsp milk

filling

225 g/8 oz cream cheese
icing sugar, to taste, plus extra for dusting
350 g/12 oz fresh summer fruits, such as red and whitecurrants, blueberries, raspberries, and small strawberries

method

1 To make the pastry, sift the flour and icing sugar into a bowl. Stir in the ground almonds. Add the butter and rub in until the mixture resembles breadcrumbs. Add the egg yolk and milk and work in with a spatula, then mix with your fingers until the dough binds together. Wrap the dough in clingfilm and chill in the refrigerator for 30 minutes.

2 On a floured work surface, roll out the pastry and use to line 12 deep tartlet or individual brioche tins. Prick the bottoms. Press a piece of foil into each tartlet, covering the edges, and bake in a preheated oven, 200°C/400°F, for 10–15 minutes or until light golden brown. Remove the foil and bake for a further 2–3 minutes. Transfer to a wire rack to cool.

3 To make the filling, place the cream cheese and icing sugar in a bowl and mix together. Place a spoonful of filling in each tartlet case and arrange the fruit on top. Dust with sifted icing sugar and serve.

apple shortcakes

ingredients

MAKES 4

2 tbsp butter, cut into small pieces, plus extra for greasing
150 g/5½ oz plain flour, plus extra for dusting
½ tsp salt
1 tsp baking powder
1 tbsp caster sugar
50 ml/2 fl oz milk
icing sugar, for dusting

filling

3 dessert apples, peeled, cored and sliced
100 g/3½ oz caster sugar
1 tbsp lemon juice
1 tsp ground cinnamon
300 ml/10 fl oz water
150 ml/5 fl oz double cream, lightly whipped

method

1 Lightly grease a baking sheet. Sift the flour, salt and baking powder into a large bowl. Stir in the sugar, then add the butter and rub it in with your fingertips until the mixture resembles fine breadcrumbs. Pour in the milk and mix to a soft dough.

2 On a lightly floured work surface, knead the dough lightly, then roll out to 1-cm/½-inch thick. Stamp out 4 circles, using a 5-cm/2-inch cutter. Transfer the circles to the prepared baking sheet.

3 Bake in a preheated oven, 220°C/425°F, for 15 minutes, until the shortcakes are well risen and lightly browned. Set aside to cool.

4 To make the filling, place the apple, sugar, lemon juice and cinnamon in a saucepan. Add the water, bring to the boil and simmer, uncovered, for 5–10 minutes or until the apples are tender. Cool slightly, then remove the apples from the pan.

5 To serve, split the shortcakes in half. Place each bottom half on an individual serving plate and spoon on a quarter of the apple slices, then the cream. Place the other half of the shortcake on top. Serve dusted with icing sugar.

raspberry éclairs

ingredients

MAKES 8

choux pastry

55 g/2 oz butter
150 ml/5 fl oz water
70 g/2½ oz plain flour, sifted
2 eggs, beaten

filling

300 ml/10 fl oz double cream
1 tbsp icing sugar
175 g/6 oz fresh raspberries

icing

115 g/4 oz icing sugar
2 tsp lemon juice
pink food colouring (optional)

method

1 To make the choux pastry, place the butter and water in a large, heavy-based saucepan and bring to the boil. Add the flour, all at once, and beat thoroughly until the mixture leaves the sides of the pan. Cool slightly, then vigorously beat in the eggs, 1 at a time.

2 Spoon the mixture into a piping bag fitted with a 1-cm/½-inch nozzle and make 8 x 7.5-cm/3-inch lengths on several dampened baking sheets. Bake in a preheated oven, 200°C/400°F, for 30 minutes or until crisp and golden. Remove from the oven and make a small hole in each éclair with the tip of a knife to let out the steam, then return to the oven for a further 5 minutes, to dry out the insides. Transfer to a wire rack to cool.

3 To make the filling, place the cream and icing sugar in a bowl and whisk until thick. Split the éclairs and fill with the cream and raspberries. To make the icing, sift the icing sugar into a bowl and stir in the lemon juice and enough water to make a smooth paste. Add pink food colouring, if desired. Drizzle the icing generously over the éclairs and allow to set before serving.

cherry & sultana rockcakes

ingredients

MAKES 10

250 g/9 oz self-raising flour
1 tsp ground allspice
6 tbsp butter, plus extra for greasing
85 g/3 oz golden caster sugar
55 g/2 oz glacé cherries, quartered
55 g/2 oz sultanas
1 egg
2 tbsp milk
raw brown sugar, for sprinkling

method

1 Sift the flour and allspice into a bowl. Add the butter and rub it in until the mixture resembles breadcrumbs. Stir in the sugar, cherries and sultanas.

2 Break the egg into a bowl and whisk in the milk. Pour most of the egg mixture into the dry ingredients and mix with a fork to make a stiff, coarse dough, adding the rest of the egg and milk, if necessary.

3 Using 2 forks, pile the mixture into 10 rocky heaps on a greased baking sheet. Sprinkle with raw brown sugar. Bake in a preheated oven, 200°C/400°F, for 10–15 minutes or until golden and firm to the touch. Cool on the baking sheet for 2 minutes, then transfer to a wire rack to cool completely.

walnut & cinnamon blondies

ingredients

MAKES 9

115 g/4 oz butter, plus extra for greasing
225 g/8 oz brown sugar
1 egg
1 egg yolk
150 g/5$^1/_2$ oz self-raising flour
1 tsp ground cinnamon
85 g/3 oz roughly chopped walnuts

method

1 Place the butter and sugar in a saucepan over low heat and stir until the sugar has dissolved. Cook, stirring, for a further 1 minute. The mixture will bubble slightly, but do not let it boil. Cool for 10 minutes.

2 Stir the egg and egg yolk into the mixture. Sift in the flour and cinnamon, add the nuts and stir until just blended. Pour the cake mixture into a greased and base-lined 18-cm/7-inch square cake tin, then bake in a preheated oven, 180°C/350°F, for 20–25 minutes or until springy in the centre and a skewer inserted into the centre of the cake comes out clean.

3 Cool in the tin for a few minutes, then run a knife round the edge of the cake to loosen it. Turn the cake out onto a wire rack and peel off the paper. Cool completely and, when cold, cut into squares.

chocolate

Chocolate is always a favourite ingredient in sweet treats, and so we've included a whole chapter especially for all you chocoholics! Your only problem will be where to begin!

Chocolate muffins go beautifully with coffee, so these are a great choice for your mid-morning break – there are four recipes to choose from, each with a special twist of its own. Mocha Cupcakes with Whipped Cream, Mocha Brownies – served either plain or with sour cream frosting – and Cappuccino Squares will also fit the bill to perfection, or perhaps a crisp Chocolate Viennese Finger or a Double Chocolate Chip Cookie or two.

For afternoon tea, go for the Caramel Chocolate Shortbread, which is sometimes called 'millionaire's shortbread'. Try it, and you'll find out why! Chocolate Butterfly Cakes are also perfect at teatime, or Tiny Chocolate Cupcakes with Ganache Frosting.

If you want a little treat in the evening, the Devil's Food Cakes with Chocolate Frosting, the Warm Molten-centred Chocolate Cupcakes and the Chocolate Tartlets – made with either plain or white chocolate – are just out of this world. At Christmas, try Panforte di Sienna, a specialty from Tuscany in Italy – it's wonderful served with a glass of dessert wine to end a festive dinner.

spiced chocolate muffins

ingredients

MAKES 12

100 g/3½ oz butter, softened
150 g/5½ oz caster sugar
115 g/4 oz brown sugar
2 large eggs
150 ml/5 fl oz sour cream
5 tbsp milk
250 g/9 oz plain flour
1 tsp bicarbonate of soda
2 tbsp cocoa powder
1 tsp allspice
200 g/7 oz plain chocolate chips

method

1 Line a 12-cup muffin pan with muffin cases.

2 Place the butter, caster sugar and brown sugar in a bowl and beat well. Beat in the eggs, sour cream and milk until thoroughly mixed. Sift the flour, bicarbonate of soda, cocoa and allspice into a separate bowl and stir into the mixture. Add the chocolate chips and mix well. Divide the mixture evenly between the paper cases. Bake in a preheated oven, 190°C/375°F, for 25–30 minutes.

3 Remove from the oven and cool for 10 minutes, then transfer to a wire rack to cool completely. Store in an airtight container until required.

double chocolate muffins

ingredients

MAKES 12

200 g/7 oz plain flour

25 g/1 oz cocoa powder, plus extra for dusting

1 tbsp baking powder

1 tsp ground cinnamon

115 g/4 oz golden caster sugar

185 g/6½ oz white chocolate, broken into pieces

2 large eggs

100 ml/3½ fl oz sunflower or peanut oil

200 ml/7 fl oz milk

method

1 Line a 12-cup muffin pan with muffin cases.

2 Sift the flour, cocoa, baking powder and cinnamon into a large mixing bowl. Stir in the sugar and 125 g/4½ oz of the white chocolate.

3 Place the eggs and oil in a separate bowl and whisk until frothy, then gradually whisk in the milk. Stir into the dry ingredients until just blended. Divide the mixture evenly between the paper cases, filling each three-quarters full. Bake in a preheated oven, 200°C/400°F, for 20 minutes or until well risen and springy to the touch. Remove the muffins from the oven, cool in the pan for 2 minutes, then transfer to a wire rack to cool completely.

4 Place the remaining white chocolate in a heatproof bowl, set the bowl over a saucepan of barely simmering water, and heat until melted. Spread over the top of the muffins. Allow to set, then dust the tops with a little cocoa and serve.

chocolate chip muffins

ingredients

MAKES 12

3 tbsp soft margarine
200 g/7 oz caster sugar
2 large eggs
150 ml/5 fl oz whole natural yogurt
5 tbsp milk
300 g/10½ oz plain flour
1 tsp bicarbonate of soda
115 g/4 oz plain chocolate chips

method

1 Line a 12-cup muffin pan with muffin cases.

2 Place the margarine and sugar in a mixing bowl and beat with a wooden spoon until light and fluffy. Beat in the eggs, yogurt and milk until combined.

3 Sift the flour and bicarbonate of soda into the mixture. Stir until just blended.

4 Stir in the chocolate chips, then divide the mixture evenly between the paper cases and bake in a preheated oven, 200°C/400°F, for 25 minutes or until risen and golden. Remove the muffins from the oven and cool in the pan for 5 minutes, then place them on a wire rack to cool completely.

chocolate orange muffins

ingredients

MAKES 9

- sunflower or peanut oil, for oiling
- 150 g/5$^1/_2$ oz self-raising white flour
- 150 g/5$^1/_2$ oz self-raising wholewheat flour
- 55 g/2 oz ground almonds
- 55 g/2 oz brown sugar
- rind and juice of 1 orange
- 175 g/6 oz cream cheese
- 2 large eggs
- 55 g/2 oz plain chocolate chips

method

1 Thoroughly oil a 9-cup muffin pan.

2 Sift both flours into a mixing bowl and stir in the ground almonds and sugar.

3 Mix the orange rind and juice, cream cheese and eggs together in a separate bowl. Make a well in the centre of the dry ingredients and stir in the wet ingredients, then add the chocolate chips. Beat well to combine all the ingredients.

4 Divide the mixture between the cups, filling each no more than three-quarters full. Bake in a preheated oven, 190°C/375°F, for 20–25 minutes or until well risen and golden brown.

5 Remove the muffins from the oven and cool slightly on a wire rack, but eat them as fresh as possible.

dark & white fudge cupcakes

ingredients

MAKES 20

200 ml/7 fl oz water
6 tbsp butter
85 g/3 oz caster sugar
1 tbsp golden syrup
3 tbsp milk
1 tsp vanilla essence
1 tsp bicarbonate of soda
225 g/8 oz plain flour
2 tbsp cocoa powder

topping

50 g/$1\frac{3}{4}$ oz plain chocolate
4 tbsp water
$3\frac{1}{2}$ tbsp butter
50 g/$1\frac{3}{4}$ oz white chocolate
350 g/12 oz icing sugar

chocolate curls

100 g/$3\frac{1}{2}$ oz plain chocolate
100 g/$3\frac{1}{2}$ oz white chocolate

method

1 Put 20 paper baking cases in 2 muffin pans, or place 20 double-layer paper cases on 2 baking sheets.

2 Put the water, butter, caster sugar and syrup in a pan. Heat gently, stirring, until the sugar has dissolved, then bring to the boil. Reduce the heat and cook gently for 5 minutes. Remove from the heat and cool.

3 Meanwhile, put the milk and vanilla essence in a bowl. Add the bicarbonate of soda and stir to dissolve. Sift the flour and cocoa into a separate bowl and add the syrup mixture. Stir in the milk and beat until smooth. Divide the mixture between the paper cases and bake the cupcakes in a preheated oven, 180ºC/350ºF, for 20 minutes or until well risen and firm to the touch. Transfer to a wire rack to cool.

4 To make the topping, break the plain chocolate into a small heatproof bowl, add half the water and half the butter, and melt over a saucepan of gently simmering water. Stir until smooth and let stand over the water. Using another bowl, repeat with the white chocolate and remaining water and butter. Sift half the sugar into each bowl and beat until smooth and thick. Top the cupcakes with the frostings and let them set. Decorate with chocolate curls made by shaving the chocolate with a potato peeler.

warm molten-centred chocolate cupcakes

ingredients

MAKES 8

4 tbsp soft margarine
55 g/2 oz caster sugar
1 large egg
85 g/3 oz self-raising flour
1 tbsp cocoa powder
55 g/2 oz plain chocolate
icing sugar, for dusting

method

1 Put 8 paper baking cases in a muffin pan, or place 8 double-layer paper cases on a baking sheet.

2 Put the margarine, sugar, egg, flour and cocoa in a large bowl and, using an electric hand whisk, beat together until just smooth.

3 Spoon half of the mixture into the paper cases. Using a teaspoon, make an indentation in the centre of each cake. Break the chocolate evenly into 8 squares and place a piece in each indentation, then spoon the remaining cake mixture on top.

4 Bake the cupcakes in a preheated oven, 190°C/375°F, for 20 minutes or until well risen and springy to the touch. Leave the cupcakes for 2–3 minutes before serving warm, dusted with sifted icing sugar.

jumbo chocolate chip cupcakes

ingredients

MAKES 8

7 tbsp soft margarine
100 g/3½ oz caster sugar
2 large eggs
100 g/3½ oz self-raising flour
100 g/3½ oz plain chocolate chips

method

1 Put 8 muffin paper cases in a muffin pan.

2 Put the margarine, sugar, eggs and flour in a large bowl and, using an electric hand whisk, beat together until just smooth. Fold in the chocolate chips. Spoon the mixture into the paper cases.

3 Bake the cupcakes in a preheated oven, 190°C/375°F, for 20–25 minutes or until well risen and golden brown. Transfer to a wire rack to cool.

mocha cupcakes with whipped cream

ingredients

MAKES 20

2 tbsp instant espresso coffee powder
6 tbsp butter
85 g/3 oz caster sugar
1 tbsp honey
200 ml/7 fl oz water
225 g/8 oz plain flour
2 tbsp cocoa powder
1 tsp bicarbonate of soda
3 tbsp milk
1 large egg, lightly beaten

topping

225 ml/8 fl oz whipping cream
cocoa powder, sifted, for dusting

method

1 Put 20 paper baking cases in 2 muffin pans, or place 20 double-layer paper cases on 2 baking sheets.

2 Put the coffee powder, butter, sugar, honey and water in a saucepan and heat gently, stirring, until the sugar has dissolved. Bring to the boil, then reduce the heat and simmer for 5 minutes. Pour into a large heatproof bowl and cool.

3 When the mixture has cooled, sift in the flour and cocoa. Dissolve the bicarbonate of soda in the milk, then add to the mixture with the egg and beat together until smooth. Spoon the mixture into the paper cases.

4 Bake the cupcakes in a preheated oven, 180°C/350°F, for 15–20 minutes or until well risen and firm to the touch. Transfer to a wire rack to cool.

5 For the topping, whisk the cream in a bowl until it holds its shape. Just before serving, spoon a heaped teaspoonful of cream on top of each cake, then dust lightly with sifted cocoa. Store the cupcakes in the refrigerator until ready to serve.

chocolate cupcakes with cream cheese frosting

ingredients

MAKES 18

6 tbsp butter, softened, or soft margarine
100 g/3½ oz caster sugar
2 eggs, lightly beaten
2 tbsp milk
55 g/2 oz plain chocolate chips
225 g/8 oz self-raising flour
25 g/1 oz cocoa powder

frosting

225 g/8 oz white chocolate
150 g/5½ oz low-fat cream cheese

method

1 Put 18 paper baking cases in 2 muffin pans, or place 18 double-layer paper cases on a baking sheet.

2 Put the butter and sugar in a bowl and beat together until light and fluffy. Gradually add the eggs, beating well after each addition. Add the milk, then fold in the chocolate chips. Sift in the flour and cocoa, then fold into the mixture. Spoon the mixture into the paper cases and smooth the tops.

3 Bake the cupcakes in a preheated oven, 200°C/400°F, for 20 minutes or until well risen and springy to the touch. Transfer to a wire rack to cool.

4 To make the frosting, break the chocolate into a small heatproof bowl and set the bowl over a saucepan of gently simmering water until melted. Cool slightly. Put the cream cheese in a bowl and beat until softened, then beat in the slightly cooled chocolate.

5 Spread a little of the frosting over the top of each cupcake, then chill in the refrigerator for 1 hour before serving.

tiny chocolate cupcakes with ganache frosting

ingredients

MAKES 20

4 tbsp butter, softened
55 g/2 oz caster sugar
1 large egg, lightly beaten
55 g/2 oz self-raising flour
2 tbsp cocoa powder
1 tbsp milk
20 chocolate-coated coffee beans, to decorate (optional)

frosting

100 g/3½ oz plain chocolate
100 ml/3½ fl oz double cream

method

1 Put 20 double-layer mini paper cases on 2 baking sheets.

2 Put the butter and sugar in a bowl and beat together until light and fluffy. Gradually beat in the egg. Sift in the flour and cocoa and then, using a metal spoon, fold them into the mixture. Stir in the milk.

3 Fill a piping bag, fitted with a large plain tip, with the mixture and pipe it into the paper cases, filling each one until half full.

4 Bake the cakes in a preheated oven, 190ºC/375ºF, for 10–15 minutes or until well risen and firm to the touch. Transfer to a wire rack to cool.

5 To make the frosting, break the chocolate into a saucepan and add the cream. Heat gently, stirring, until the chocolate has melted. Pour into a large heatproof bowl and, using an electric hand whisk, beat the mixture for 10 minutes or until thick, glossy and cool.

6 Fill a piping bag, fitted with a large star tip, with the frosting and pipe a swirl on top of each cupcake. Alternatively, spoon over the frosting. Chill in the refrigerator for 1 hour before serving. Serve decorated with a chocolate-coated coffee bean, if liked.

devil's food cakes with chocolate frosting

ingredients

MAKES 18

3½ tbsp soft margarine
115 g/4 oz brown sugar
2 large eggs
115 g/4 oz plain flour
½ tsp bicarbonate of soda
25 g/1 oz cocoa powder
125 ml/4 fl oz sour cream

frosting

125 g/4½ oz plain chocolate
2 tbsp caster sugar
150 ml/5 fl oz sour cream

chocolate curls

(optional)
100 g/3½ oz plain chocolate

method

1 Put 18 paper baking cases in a muffin pan, or put 18 double-layer paper cases on a baking sheet.

2 Put the margarine, sugar, eggs, flour, bicarbonate of soda and cocoa in a large bowl and, using an electric hand whisk, beat together until just smooth. Using a metal spoon, fold in the sour cream. Spoon the mixture into the paper cases.

3 Bake the cupcakes in a preheated oven, 180°C/350°F, for 20 minutes or until well risen and firm to the touch. Transfer to a wire rack to cool.

4 To make the frosting, break the chocolate into a heatproof bowl. Set the bowl over a saucepan of gently simmering water and heat until melted, stirring occasionally. Remove from the heat and cool slightly, then whisk in the sugar and sour cream until combined. Spread the frosting over the tops of the cupcakes and set in the refrigerator before serving. If liked, serve decorated with chocolate curls made by shaving plain chocolate with a potato peeler.

chocolate butterfly cakes

ingredients

MAKES 12

8 tbsp soft margarine
100 g/3½ oz caster sugar
150 g/5½ oz self-raising flour
2 large eggs
2 tbsp cocoa powder
25 g/1 oz plain chocolate, melted
icing sugar, for dusting

filling

6 tbsp butter, softened
175 g/6 oz icing sugar
25 g/1 oz plain chocolate, melted

method

1 Put 12 paper baking cases in a muffin pan, or put 12 double-layer paper cases on a baking sheet.

2 Put the margarine, sugar, flour, eggs and cocoa in a large bowl and, using an electric hand whisk, beat together until just smooth. Beat in the melted chocolate. Spoon the mixture into the paper cases, filling them three-quarters full.

3 Bake the cupcakes in a preheated oven, 180°C/350°F, for 15 minutes or until springy to the touch. Transfer to a wire rack to cool completely.

4 To make the filling, put the butter in a bowl and beat until fluffy. Sift in the icing sugar and beat together until smooth. Add the melted chocolate and beat until well mixed.

5 When the cupcakes are cold, use a serrated knife to cut a circle from the top of each cake and then cut each circle in half. Spread or pipe a little of the buttercream into the centre of each cupcake and press the 2 semicircular halves into it at an angle to resemble butterfly wings. Dust with a little sifted icing sugar before serving.

mocha brownies

ingredients

MAKES 16

55 g/2 oz butter, plus extra for greasing
115 g/4 oz plain chocolate, broken into pieces
175 g/6 oz brown sugar
2 eggs
1 tbsp instant coffee powder, dissolved in 1 tbsp hot water, cooled
85 g/3 oz plain flour
1/2 tsp baking powder
55 g/2 oz roughly chopped pecan nuts

method

1 Grease and line the bottom of a 20-cm/8-inch square cake tin. Place the butter and chocolate in a heavy-based saucepan over low heat until melted. Stir and set aside to cool.

2 Place the sugar and eggs in a large bowl and cream together until light and fluffy. Fold in the chocolate mixture and cooled coffee and mix thoroughly. Sift in the flour and baking powder and lightly fold into the mixture, then carefully fold in the pecan nuts.

3 Pour the mixture into the prepared tin and bake in a preheated oven, 180°C/350°F, for 25–30 minutes or until firm and a skewer inserted into the centre comes out clean.

4 Cool in the tin for a few minutes, then run a knife round the edge of the cake to loosen it. Turn the cake out onto a wire rack and peel off the lining paper. Cool completely and when cold, cut into squares.

mocha brownies with sour cream frosting

ingredients

MAKES 9 LARGE OR 16 SMALL BROWNIES

55 g/2 oz butter, plus extra for greasing
115 g/4 oz plain chocolate, broken into pieces
175 g/6 oz dark brown sugar
2 eggs
2 tbsp strong coffee, cooled
85 g/3 oz plain flour
½ tsp baking powder
pinch of salt
55 g/2 oz shelled walnuts, chopped

frosting

115 g/4 oz plain chocolate, broken into pieces
150 ml/5 fl oz sour cream

method

1 Place the butter and chocolate in a small heatproof bowl and set over a saucepan of gently simmering water until melted. Stir until smooth. Remove from the heat and cool.

2 Beat the sugar and eggs together until pale and thick. Fold in the chocolate mixture and coffee. Mix well. Sift the flour, baking powder and salt into the cake mixture and fold in. Fold in the walnuts. Pour the cake mixture into a greased 20-cm/8-inch square cake tin base-lined with baking parchment and bake in a preheated oven, 180°C/350°F, for 20–25 minutes or until set. Cool in the tin.

3 To make the frosting, melt the chocolate. Stir in the sour cream and beat until evenly blended. Spoon the topping over the brownies and make a swirling pattern with a spatula. Leave to set in a cool place. Cut into squares, then remove from the tin and serve.

cappuccino squares

ingredients

MAKES 15

225 g/8 oz butter, softened, plus extra for greasing
225 g/8 oz self-raising flour
1 tsp baking powder
1 tsp cocoa powder, plus extra for dusting
225 g/8 oz golden caster sugar
4 eggs, beaten
3 tbsp instant coffee powder, dissolved in 2 tbsp hot water

white chocolate frosting

115 g/4 oz white chocolate, broken into pieces
55 g/2 oz butter, softened
3 tbsp milk
175 g/6 oz icing sugar

method

1 Grease and line the bottom of a shallow 28 x 18-cm/11 x 7-inch tin. Sift the flour, baking powder and cocoa into a bowl and add the butter, caster sugar, eggs and coffee. Beat well, by hand or with an electric whisk, until smooth, then spoon into the tin and smooth the top.

2 Bake in a preheated oven, 180°C/350°F, for 35–40 minutes or until risen and firm. Cool in the tin for 10 minutes, then turn out onto a wire rack, peel off the lining paper and cool completely. To make the frosting, place the chocolate, butter and milk in a bowl set over a saucepan of simmering water and stir until the chocolate has melted.

3 Remove the bowl from the pan and sift in the icing sugar. Beat until smooth, then spread over the cake. Dust the top of the cake with sifted cocoa, then cut into squares.

panforte di siena

ingredients

SERVES 12–16

butter, for greasing
55 g/2 oz glacé cherries, quartered
115 g/4 oz mixed candied orange and lemon peel, finely chopped
2 tbsp candied ginger, roughly chopped
115 g/4 oz flaked almonds
115 g/4 oz hazelnuts, toasted and coarsely ground
55 g/2 oz plain flour
25 g/1 oz cocoa powder
1 tsp ground cinnamon
1/4 tsp ground cloves
1/4 tsp ground nutmeg
1/4 tsp ground coriander
115 g/4 oz honey
115 g/4 oz golden caster sugar
1 tsp orange-flower water
icing sugar, for dusting

method

1 Thoroughly grease the bottom of a 20-cm/8-inch loose-based cake or tart tin. Line the bottom with non-stick baking parchment. Place the cherries, candied peel, ginger, almonds and hazelnuts in a bowl. Sift in the flour, cocoa, cinnamon, cloves, nutmeg and coriander and mix. Set aside.

2 Place the honey, sugar and orange flower water in a saucepan and heat gently until the sugar has dissolved. Bring the mixture to the boil and boil steadily until a temperature of 116°C/241°F has been reached on a sugar thermometer, or a small amount of the mixture forms a soft ball when dropped into cold water.

3 Quickly remove the pan from the heat and stir in the dry ingredients. Mix thoroughly and turn into the prepared tin. Spread evenly and bake in a preheated oven, 160°C/325°F, for 30 minutes. Cool in the pan, then turn out and carefully peel away the lining paper. Dust icing sugar lightly over the top and cut into wedges to serve.

chocolate tartlets

ingredients

MAKES 4

10 oz/275 g ready-made sweet pastry

150 g/5½ oz bittersweet chocolate, broken into pieces

50 g/1¾ oz butter

100 ml/3½ fl oz whipping cream

1 large egg

25 g/1 oz caster sugar

cocoa powder and chocolate curls, to decorate

crème fraîche, to serve

method

1 Roll out the pastry and use to line 4 x 12-cm/ 4½-inch fluted tart tins with removable bases. Line the pastry cases with waxed paper, then fill with baking beans. Place on a preheated baking sheet and bake in a preheated oven, 200°C/400°F, for 5 minutes or until the pastry rims look set. Remove the paper and beans and return the pastry shells to the oven for 5 minutes or until the bases look dry. Remove from the oven, then set aside on the baking sheet. Reduce the oven temperature to 180°C/350°F.

2 Meanwhile, place the chocolate in a bowl set over a saucepan of simmering water so that the bowl does not touch the water. Add the butter and cream and heat until the chocolate and butter melt. Remove from the heat.

3 Beat the egg and sugar together until light and fluffy. Stir the melted chocolate mixture until smooth, then stir it into the egg mixture. Carefully pour the filling into the tart cases, then transfer to the oven and bake for 15 minutes or until the filling is set and the pastry is golden brown. If the pastry looks as though it is becoming too brown, cover it with foil.

4 Transfer the tartlets to a wire rack to cool completely. Dust with cocoa powder, decorate with chocolate curls, and serve with the crème fraîche.

white chocolate tarts

ingredients

MAKES 12

225 g/8 oz plain flour, plus extra for dusting
2 tbsp golden caster sugar
150 g/5½ oz chilled butter, diced
2 egg yolks
2 tbsp cold water
plain chocolate curls, to decorate (see page 80)
cocoa powder, for dusting

filling

1 vanilla bean
400 ml/14 fl oz double cream
350 g/12 oz white chocolate, broken into pieces

method

1 Place the flour and sugar in a bowl. Add the butter and rub it in until the mixture resembles fine breadcrumbs. Place the egg yolks and water in a separate bowl and mix together. Stir into the dry ingredients and mix to form a dough. Knead for 1 minute, or until smooth. Wrap in clingfilm and chill for 20 minutes.

2 Roll out the dough on a floured work surface and use to line 12 tartlet tins. Prick the bases, cover and chill for 15 minutes. Line the cases with foil and baking beans and bake in a preheated oven, 200°C/400°F, for 10 minutes. Remove the beans and foil and cook for a further 5 minutes. Set aside to cool.

3 To make the filling, split the vanilla bean lengthways and scrape out the black seeds with a knife. Place the seeds in a saucepan with the cream and heat until almost boiling. Place the chocolate in a heatproof bowl and pour over the hot cream. Keep stirring until smooth. Whisk the mixture with an electric whisk until thickened and the whisk leaves a trail when lifted. Chill in the refrigerator for 30 minutes, then whisk until soft peaks form. Divide the filling between the pastry shells and chill for 30 minutes. Decorate with chocolate curls and dust with cocoa powder.

caramel chocolate shortbread

ingredients

MAKES 12

115 g/4 oz butter, plus extra for greasing
175 g/6 oz plain flour
55 g/2 oz golden caster sugar

filling and topping

175 g/6 oz butter
115 g/4 oz golden caster sugar
3 tbsp golden syrup
400 g/14 oz canned condensed milk
200 g/7 oz plain chocolate, broken into pieces

method

1 Grease and line the bottom of a 23-cm/9-inch shallow square cake tin. Place the butter, flour and sugar in a food processor and process until it starts to bind together. Press into the pan and level the top. Bake in a preheated oven, 180°C/350°F, for 20–25 minutes or until golden.

2 Meanwhile, make the caramel. Place the butter, sugar, syrup and condensed milk in a heavy-based saucepan. Heat gently until the sugar has melted. Bring to the boil, then reduce the heat and simmer for 6–8 minutes, stirring, until very thick. Pour over the shortbread and chill in the refrigerator for 2 hours, or until firm.

3 Melt the chocolate and allow to cool a little, then spread over the caramel. Chill in the refrigerator for 2 hours, or until set. Cut the shortbread into 12 pieces using a sharp knife and serve.

refrigerator cake

ingredients

MAKES 12 PIECES

55 g/2 oz butter, plus extra for greasing
55 g/2 oz raisins
2 tbsp brandy
115 g/4 oz plain chocolate, broken into pieces
115 g/4 oz milk chocolate, broken into pieces
2 tbsp golden syrup
175 g/6 oz digestive biscuits, roughly broken
55 g/2 oz flaked almonds, lightly toasted
25 g/1 oz glacé cherries, chopped

topping

100 g/3½ oz plain chocolate, broken into pieces
20 g/¾ oz butter

method

1 Grease and line the bottom of an 18-cm/7-inch shallow square cake tin. Place the raisins and brandy in a bowl and soak for 30 minutes. Put the chocolate, butter and golden syrup in a saucepan and heat gently until melted.

2 Stir in the digestives, almonds, cherries, raisins and brandy. Turn into the prepared tin and cool, then cover and chill in the refrigerator for 1 hour.

3 To make the topping, place the chocolate and butter in a small heatproof bowl and melt over a saucepan of gently simmering water. Stir and pour the chocolate mixture over the biscuit base. Chill in the refrigerator for 8 hours, or overnight. Cut into bars or squares to serve.

no-bake chocolate squares

ingredients

MAKES 16

275 g/9½ oz plain chocolate
175 g/6 oz butter
4 tbsp golden syrup
2 tbsp dark rum (optional)
175 g/6 oz plain biscuits
25 g/1 oz toasted rice cereal
50 g/1¾ oz chopped walnuts or pecan nuts
100 g/3½ oz glacé cherries, roughly chopped
25 g/1 oz white chocolate, to decorate

method

1 Line an 18-cm/7-inch square cake tin with baking parchment. Place the plain chocolate in a large bowl with the butter, syrup and rum, if using, and set over a saucepan of gently simmering water, stirring constantly until melted and blended.

2 Break the biscuits into small pieces and stir into the chocolate mixture with the rice cereal, nuts and cherries.

3 Pour the mixture into the tin and level the top, pressing down well with the back of a spoon. Chill in the refrigerator for 2 hours.

4 To decorate, melt the white chocolate and drizzle it over the top of the cake in a random pattern. Leave to set. To serve, carefully turn out of the tin and remove the baking parchment. Cut into 16 squares and serve.

chocolate viennese fingers

ingredients

MAKES ABOUT 30

115 g/4 oz butter, softened, plus extra for greasing

55 g/2 oz golden icing sugar, sifted

125 g/4½ oz plain flour

1 tbsp cocoa powder

100 g/3½ oz plain chocolate, melted and cooled

method

1 Beat the butter and sugar together until light and fluffy. Sift the flour and cocoa powder into the bowl and work the mixture until it is a smooth, piping consistency.

2 Spoon into a large piping bag fitted with a 2.5-cm/1-inch fluted tip. Pipe 6-cm/2½-inch lengths of the mixture onto 2 greased baking sheets, allowing room for expansion during cooking. Bake in a preheated oven, 180°C/350°F, for 15 minutes or until firm.

3 Cool on the baking sheets for 2 minutes, then transfer to a wire rack to cool completely. Dip the ends of the biscuits into the melted chocolate and allow to set before serving.

double chocolate chip cookies

ingredients

MAKES 12

200 g/7 oz butter, softened, plus extra for greasing
200 g/7 oz golden caster sugar
1/2 tsp vanilla essence
1 large egg
225 g/8 oz plain flour
pinch of salt
1 tsp bicarbonate of soda
115 g/4 oz white chocolate chips
115 g/4 oz plain chocolate chips

method

1 Place the butter, sugar and vanilla essence in a large bowl and beat together. Gradually beat in the egg until the mixture is light and fluffy.

2 Sift the flour, salt and bicarbonate of soda over the mixture and fold in. Fold in the chocolate chips. Drop dessertspoonfuls of the mixture onto 3 greased baking sheets, spaced well apart to allow for spreading during cooking.

3 Bake in a preheated oven, 180°C/350°F, for 10–12 minutes or until crisp outside but still soft inside. Cool on the baking sheets for 2 minutes, then transfer to wire racks to cool completely.

special occasions

This is where you can really give your creative streak a free rein and have endless fun. There are fabulous recipes here to help you celebrate a wedding, a birth, a birthday, an anniversary or one of the festive occasions in the year.

Children love novelty, so get them involved and make special cupcakes decorated for Easter, Halloween or Christmas. For their birthday parties, serve Birthday Party Cupcakes, Lemon Butterfly Cakes, Gingerbread People and Party Biscuits decorated with colourful sugar-coated chocolate beans – these will render the party guests speechless just long enough for you to catch your breath!

When romance is in the air, make Valentine Heart Cupcakes for your loved one, or use a biscuit cutter to shape Vanilla Hearts. A Cupcake-Wedding-Cake is perfect for an informal wedding, and to celebrate both weddings and the subsequent anniversaries, choose Rose Petal Muffins and Cupcakes and Strawberry Rose Meringues – they look, and taste, absolutely stunning. And for a Christening – Christening Cupcakes with pale pink and pale blue icing, of course!

For an adult birthday party or just a get-together, be a little different and serve muffins laced with your favourite liqueur – brandy, Amaretto, Cointreau, the choice is yours.

rose petal muffins

ingredients

MAKES 12

1 tbsp sunflower or peanut oil, for oiling (if using)
225 g/8 oz plain flour
2 tsp baking powder
pinch of salt
4 tbsp butter
6 tbsp caster sugar
1 large egg, beaten
110 ml/4 fl oz milk
1 tsp rose water
50 g/1³/₄ oz edible rose petals, rinsed, patted dry and lightly snipped

rose petal icing

100 g/3¹/₂ oz icing sugar
1 tbsp liquid glucose
1 tbsp rose water
50 g/1³/₄ oz edible rose petals, rinsed and patted dry

method

1 Oil a 12-cup muffin pan with sunflower oil, or line it with 12 muffin paper cases. Sift the flour, baking powder and salt into a large mixing bowl.

2 In a separate large bowl, cream together the butter and caster sugar, then stir in the beaten egg, milk, rose water and snipped rose petals. Add the butter mixture to the flour mixture and then gently stir together until just combined. Do not overstir the mixture – it is fine for it to be a little lumpy.

3 Divide the muffin mixture evenly between the 12 cups in the muffin pan or the paper cases (they should be about two-thirds full). Transfer to a preheated oven, 200°C/400°F, and bake for 20 minutes or until risen and golden.

4 While the muffins are cooking, make the icing. Place the icing sugar in a bowl, then stir in the liquid glucose and rose water. Cover with clingfilm until ready to use.

5 When the muffins are cooked, remove them from the oven and place on a wire rack to cool. When they have cooled, spread each muffin with some of the icing, strew over and/or around with the rose petals and serve.

frosted lavender muffins

ingredients

MAKES 12

1 large baking apple, peeled, cored and thinly sliced
3 tbsp water
150 g/5½ oz plain flour
1 tsp baking powder
1 tsp bicarbonate of soda
pinch of salt
4 tbsp butter
4 tbsp caster sugar
1 large egg, beaten
½ tsp vanilla essence
1 tbsp dried lavender flowers, stripped from their stalks

lavender icing

100 g/3½ oz icing sugar
1 tbsp dried lavender flowers
1 tbsp liquid glucose
1–2 tbsp milk

method

1 The day before you make the muffins, place the icing sugar in a bowl, then add the dried lavender flowers. Cover with clingfilm and leave overnight until ready for use.

2 To make the muffins, place the sliced apple and water in a saucepan and bring to the boil, then cover and simmer for 15–20 minutes, stirring occasionally, until the water has been absorbed. Remove from the heat and cool. Process in a food processor until smooth.

3 Line a 12-cup muffin pan with paper cases. Sift the flour, baking powder, bicarbonate of soda and salt into a mixing bowl. In a separate bowl, cream together the butter and caster sugar, then stir in the beaten egg, vanilla essence, apple purée and dried lavender flowers. Stir the egg mixture into the flour mixture until just combined. Do not overstir the mixture – it is fine for it to be a little lumpy.

4 Divide the muffin mixture between the paper cases (they should be about two-thirds full). Transfer to a preheated oven, 200°C/400°F, and bake for 20 minutes or until risen and golden. Cool completely on a wire rack.

5 To finish making the icing, sift the sugar/lavender mixture into a bowl and discard the flowers. Stir in the liquid glucose and enough milk to make the icing easy to spread. Spread each muffin with icing and serve.

irish coffee muffins

ingredients

MAKES 12

1 tbsp sunflower or peanut oil, for oiling (if using)
275 g/10 oz plain flour
1 tbsp baking powder
pinch of salt
85 g/3 oz butter
55 g/2 oz raw sugar
1 large egg, beaten
125 ml/4 fl oz double cream
1 tsp almond essence
2 tbsp strong coffee
2 tbsp coffee-flavoured liqueur
4 tbsp Irish whiskey
whipped double cream, to serve (optional)

method

1 Oil a 12-cup muffin pan with sunflower oil, or line it with 12 muffin paper cases. Sift the flour, baking powder and salt into a large mixing bowl.

2 In a separate large bowl, cream the butter and raw sugar together, then stir in the beaten egg. Pour in the double cream, almond essence, coffee, liqueur and whiskey and stir together. Add the whiskey mixture to the flour mixture and then gently stir together until just combined. Do not overstir the mixture – it is fine for it to be a little lumpy.

3 Divide the muffin mixture evenly between the 12 cups in the muffin pan or the paper cases (they should be about two-thirds full). Transfer to a preheated oven, 200°C/400°F, and bake for 20 minutes or until risen and golden. Remove the muffins from the oven and serve warm, or place them on a wire rack to cool. If liked, fill the muffins with whipped double cream, to serve.

mocha muffins

ingredients

MAKES 12

1 tbsp sunflower or peanut oil, for oiling (if using)
225 g/8 oz plain flour
1 tbsp baking powder
2 tbsp cocoa powder
pinch of salt
115 g/4 oz butter, melted
150 g/5½ oz raw sugar
1 large egg, beaten
110 ml/4 fl oz milk
1 tsp almond essence
2 tbsp strong coffee
1 tbsp instant coffee powder
55 g/2 oz plain chocolate chips
25 g/1 oz raisins

cocoa topping

3 tbsp raw sugar
1 tbsp cocoa powder
1 tsp allspice

method

1 Oil a 12-cup muffin pan with sunflower oil, or line it with 12 muffin paper cases. Sift the flour, baking powder, cocoa and salt into a large mixing bowl.

2 In a separate large bowl, cream the butter and raw sugar together, then stir in the beaten egg. Pour in the milk, almond essence and coffee, then add the coffee powder, chocolate chips and raisins and gently mix together. Add the raisin mixture to the flour mixture and stir together until just combined. Do not overstir the mixture – it is fine for it to be a little lumpy.

3 Divide the muffin mixture evenly between the 12 cups in the muffin pan or the paper cases (they should be about two-thirds full). To make the topping, place the raw sugar in a bowl, add the cocoa and allspice and mix together well. Sprinkle the topping over the muffins, then transfer to a preheated oven, 190°C/375°F, and bake for 20 minutes or until risen and golden. Remove the muffins from the oven and serve warm, or place them on a wire rack to cool.

triple chocolate muffins

ingredients

MAKES 12

225 g/8 oz plain flour
25 g/1 oz cocoa powder
2 tsp baking powder
1/2 tsp bicarbonate of soda
100 g/3 1/2 oz plain chocolate chips
100 g/3 1/2 oz white chocolate chips
2 large eggs, beaten
300 ml/10 fl oz sour cream
85 g/3 oz brown sugar
85 g/3 oz butter, melted

method

1 Line a 12-cup muffin pan with muffin paper cases. Sift the flour, cocoa, baking powder and bicarbonate of soda into a large bowl, add the plain and white chocolate chips, and stir.

2 Place the eggs, sour cream, sugar and melted butter in a separate mixing bowl and mix well. Add the wet ingredients to the dry ingredients and stir gently until just combined.

3 Divide the mixture between the paper cases and bake in a preheated oven, 200°C/400°F, for 20 minutes or until well risen and firm to the touch. Remove from the oven and serve warm, or place on a wire rack to cool.

rice muffins with amaretto

ingredients

MAKES 9

butter, for greasing
150 g/5½ oz plain flour
1 tbsp baking powder
½ tsp bicarbonate of soda
½ tsp salt
1 large egg
4 tbsp honey
110 ml/4 fl oz milk
2 tbsp sunflower or peanut oil
½ tsp almond essence
55 g/2 oz cooked risotto rice
2–3 Amaretti biscuits, roughly crushed

amaretto butter

1 tbsp honey
1–2 tbsp Amaretto
100 g/3½ oz Mascarpone cheese

method

1 Grease 9 cups of a 12-cup muffin pan with butter. Sift the flour, baking powder, bicarbonate of soda and salt into a large bowl and stir. Make a well in the centre.

2 In a separate bowl, beat the egg, honey, milk, oil and almond essence with an electric whisk for about 2 minutes or until light and foamy. Gradually beat in the rice. Pour into the well in the dry ingredients and, using a fork, stir lightly until just combined.

3 Divide the mixture evenly between the 9 cups in the muffin pan. Sprinkle each muffin with Amaretti crumbs and bake in a preheated oven, 200°C/400°F, for 15 minutes or until risen and golden. The tops should spring back when pressed. Remove from the oven and cool in the pan for about 1 minute. Carefully remove the muffins and cool slightly.

4 To make the Amaretto butter, place the honey, Amaretto and Mascarpone in a small bowl and beat together. Spoon into a small serving bowl and serve with the warm muffins.

brandied cherry muffins

ingredients

MAKES 12

1 tbsp sunflower or peanut oil, for oiling (if using)
225 g/8 oz plain flour
1 tbsp baking powder
pinch of salt
3 tbsp butter
2 tbsp caster sugar
1 large egg, beaten
200 ml/7 fl oz milk
2 tsp cherry brandy
300 g/10½ oz drained canned cherries, chopped

method

1 Oil a 12-cup muffin pan with sunflower oil, or line it with 12 muffin paper cases. Sift the flour, baking powder and salt into a large mixing bowl.

2 In a separate large bowl, cream the butter and caster sugar together, then stir in the beaten egg. Pour in the milk and cherry brandy, then add the chopped cherries and gently stir together. Add the cherry mixture to the flour mixture, then gently stir together until just combined. Do not overstir the mixture – it is fine for it to be a little lumpy.

3 Divide the muffin mixture between the 12 cups in the muffin pan or the paper cases (they should be about two-thirds full). Transfer to a preheated oven, 200°C/400°F, and bake for 20–25 minutes or until risen and golden. Remove from the oven and serve warm, or place them on a wire rack to cool.

apricot muffins with cointreau

ingredients

MAKES 12

1 tbsp sunflower or peanut oil, for oiling (if using)
125 g/4½ oz self-raising flour
2 tsp baking powder
175 g/6 oz butter
125 g/4½ oz caster sugar
2 large eggs, beaten
110 ml/4 fl oz milk
4 tbsp single cream
1 tbsp orange-flavoured liqueur, such as Cointreau
85 g/3 oz no-soak dried apricots, chopped
85 g/3 oz no-soak dried dates, pitted and chopped

cinnamon topping

3 tbsp raw sugar
1 tsp ground cinnamon
1 tbsp freshly grated orange rind

method

1 Oil a 12-cup muffin pan with sunflower oil, or line it with 12 muffin paper cases.

2 Sift the flour and baking powder into a large mixing bowl.

3 In a separate large bowl, cream together the butter and caster sugar, then stir in the beaten eggs. Pour in the milk, cream and orange-flavoured liqueur, then add the chopped apricots and dates and gently mix together. Add the fruit mixture to the flour mixture and then gently stir together until just combined. Do not overstir the mixture – it is fine for it to be a little lumpy.

4 Divide the muffin mixture evenly between the 12 cups in the muffin pan or the paper cases (they should be about two-thirds full). To make the topping, place the raw sugar in a small bowl, then mix in the cinnamon and orange rind. Sprinkle the topping over the muffins, then transfer to the oven and bake in a preheated oven, 190°C/375°F, for 20 minutes or until risen and golden. Remove the muffins from the oven and serve warm, or place them on a wire rack to cool.

marshmallow muffins

ingredients

MAKES 12

70 g/2½ oz butter
275 g/10 oz plain flour
6 tbsp cocoa powder
3 tsp baking powder
85 g/3 oz caster sugar
100 g/3½ oz milk chocolate chips
55 g/2 oz multicoloured mini marshmallows
1 large egg, beaten
300 ml/10 fl oz milk

method

1 Line a 12-cup muffin pan with muffin paper cases. Melt the butter in a pan.

2 Sift the flour, cocoa and baking powder together into a large bowl. Stir in the sugar, chocolate chips and marshmallows until thoroughly mixed.

3 Whisk the egg, milk and melted butter together in a separate bowl, then gently stir into the flour to form a stiff mixture. Divide the mixture evenly between the muffin liners.

4 Bake in a preheated oven, 190°C/375°F, for 20–25 minutes or until well risen and golden brown. Remove from the oven and cool in the pan for 5 minutes, then place on a wire rack to cool completely.

easter cupcakes

ingredients

MAKES 12

8 tbsp butter, softened, or soft margarine
115 g/4 oz caster sugar
2 eggs, lightly beaten
85 g/3 oz self-raising flour
25 g/1 oz cocoa powder

topping

6 tbsp butter, softened
175 g/6 oz icing sugar
1 tbsp milk
2–3 drops of vanilla essence
36 mini sugar-coated chocolate eggs

method

1 Put 12 paper baking cases in a muffin pan, or place 12 double-layer paper cases on a baking sheet.

2 Put the butter and sugar in a bowl and beat together until light and fluffy. Gradually add the eggs, beating well after each addition. Sift in the flour and cocoa and, using a large metal spoon, fold into the mixture. Spoon the mixture into the paper cases.

3 Bake the cupcakes in a preheated oven, 180°C/350°F, for 15–20 minutes or until well risen and firm to the touch. Transfer to a wire rack to cool.

4 To make the buttercream topping, put the butter in a bowl and beat until fluffy. Sift in the icing sugar and beat together until well mixed, adding the milk and vanilla essence.

5 When the cupcakes are cold, put the frosting in a piping bag fitted with a large star tip and pipe a circle around the edge of each cupcake to form a nest. Place 3 chocolate eggs in the centre of each nest, to decorate.

halloween cupcakes

ingredients

MAKES 12

8 tbsp soft margarine
115 g/4 oz caster sugar
2 eggs
115 g/4 oz self-raising flour

topping

200 g/7 oz orange ready-to-roll coloured fondant icing
icing sugar, for dusting
55 g/2 oz black ready-to-roll coloured fondant icing
black cake writing icing
white cake writing icing

method

1 Put 12 paper baking cases in a muffin pan, or place 12 double-layer paper cases on a baking sheet.

2 Put the margarine, sugar, eggs and flour in a bowl and, using an electric hand whisk, beat together until smooth. Spoon the mixture into the cases.

3 Bake the cupcakes in a preheated oven, 180°C/350°F, for 15–20 minutes or until well risen, golden brown and firm to the touch. Transfer to a wire rack to cool.

4 Knead the orange icing until pliable, then roll out on a work surface dusted with icing sugar. Using the palm of your hand, lightly rub icing sugar into the icing to prevent it from spotting. Using a 5.5-cm/2¼-inch plain round cutter, cut out 12 circles, rerolling the icing as necessary. Place a circle on top of each cupcake.

5 Roll out the black icing on a work surface lightly dusted with icing sugar. Using the palm of your hand, lightly rub icing sugar into the icing to prevent it from spotting. Using a 3-cm/1¼-inch plain round cutter, cut out 12 circles and place them on the centre of the cupcakes. Using black writing icing, pipe 8 legs on to each spider and using white writing icing, draw 2 eyes and a mouth.

christmas cupcakes

ingredients

MAKES 16

9 tbsp butter, softened
200 g/7 oz caster sugar
4–6 drops almond essence
4 eggs, lightly beaten
150 g/5½ oz self-raising flour
175 g/6 oz ground almonds

topping

450 g/1 lb white ready-to-roll fondant icing
55 g/2 oz green ready-to-roll coloured fondant icing
25 g/1 oz red ready-to-roll coloured fondant icing
icing sugar, for dusting

method

1 Put 16 paper muffin cases in a muffin pan.

2 Put the butter, sugar and almond essence in a bowl and beat together until light and fluffy. Gradually add the eggs, beating well after each addition. Add the flour and, using a large metal spoon, fold it into the mixture, then fold in the ground almonds. Spoon the mixture into the paper cases to half-fill them.

3 Bake the cakes in a preheated oven, 180ºC/350ºF, for 20 minutes or until well risen, golden brown and firm to the touch. Transfer to a wire rack to cool.

4 When the cakes are cold, knead the white icing until pliable, then roll out on a work surface lightly dusted with icing sugar. Using a 7-cm/2¾-inch plain round cutter, cut out 16 circles, rerolling the icing as necessary. Place a circle on top of each cupcake.

5 Roll out the green icing on a work surface lightly dusted with icing sugar. Using the palm of your hand, rub icing sugar into the frosting to prevent it from spotting. Using a holly leaf-shaped cutter, cut out 32 leaves, rerolling the icing as necessary. Brush each leaf with a little cooled boiled water and place 2 leaves on top of each cake. Roll the red icing between the palms of your hands to form 48 berries and place in the centre of the leaves.

valentine heart cupcakes

ingredients

MAKES 6

6 tbsp butter, softened, or soft margarine
85 g/3 oz caster sugar
1/2 tsp vanilla essence
2 eggs, lightly beaten
70 g/2 1/2 oz plain flour
1 tbsp cocoa powder
1 tsp baking powder

marzipan hearts

35 g/1 1/4 oz marzipan
red food colouring (liquid or paste)
icing sugar, for dusting

topping

4 tbsp butter, softened
115 g/4 oz icing sugar
25 g/1 oz plain chocolate, melted
6 chocolate flower decorations

method

1 To make the hearts, knead the marzipan until pliable, then add a few drops of red colouring and knead until evenly coloured red. Roll out the marzipan to a thickness of 5 mm/ 1/4 inch on a work surface dusted with icing sugar. Using a small heart-shaped cutter, cut out 6 hearts. Place on a tray lined with waxed paper and dusted with icing sugar. Set asie to dry for 3–4 hours.

2 Put 6 paper muffin cases in a muffin pan.

3 Put the butter, sugar and vanilla essence in a bowl and beat together until light and fluffy. Gradually add the eggs, beating well after each addition. Sift in the flour, cocoa and baking powder and, using a large metal spoon, fold into the mixture. Spoon the mixture into the paper cases.

4 Bake the cupcakes in a preheated oven, 180°C/350°F, for 20–25 minutes or until well risen and firm to the touch. Transfer to a wire rack to cool.

5 To make the topping, put the butter in a large bowl and beat until fluffy. Sift in the icing sugar and beat together until smooth. Add the melted chocolate and beat together until well mixed. When the cakes are cold, spread a little frosting on top of each cake and decorate with a chocolate flower.

cupcake wedding cake

ingredients

MAKES 48

450 g/1 lb butter, softened
450 g/1 lb caster sugar
2 tsp vanilla essence
8 large eggs, lightly beaten
450 g/1 lb self-raising flour
150 ml/5 fl oz milk

topping

550 g/1 lb 4 oz icing sugar
48 ready-made sugar roses, or 48 small fresh rosebuds gently rinsed and left to dry on kitchen paper

to assemble the cake

one 50-cm/20-inch, one 40-cm/16-inch, one 30-cm/12-inch and one 20-cm/8-inch sandblasted glass disk with polished edges, or 4 silver cake boards
13 white or Perspex cake pillars
1 small bouquet of fresh flowers in a small vase

method

1 Put 48 paper baking cases in a muffin pan, or place 48 double-layer paper cases on a baking sheet.

2 Put the butter, sugar and vanilla essence in a bowl and beat together until light and fluffy. Gradually add the eggs, beating well after each addition. Add the flour and, using a large metal spoon, fold into the mixture with the milk. Spoon the mixture into the paper cases.

3 Bake the cupcakes in a preheated oven, 180°C/350°F, for 15–20 minutes or until well risen and firm to the touch. Transfer to a wire rack to cool.

4 To make the topping, sift the icing sugar into a large bowl. Add 3–4 tablespoons hot water and stir until the mixture is smooth and thick enough to coat the back of a wooden spoon. Spoon a little on top of each cupcake. Store in an airtight container for up to one day.

5 On the day of serving, carefully place a sugar rose or rosebud on top of each cupcake. To arrange the cupcakes, place the largest disk or board on a table where the finished display is to be. Stand 5 pillars on the disk and arrange some of the cupcakes on the base. Continue with the remaining bases, pillars (using only 4 pillars to support each remaining tier), and cupcakes to make 4 tiers, standing the bouquet of flowers in the centre of the top tier.

rose petal cupcakes

ingredients

MAKES 12

8 tbsp butter, softened
115 g/4 oz caster sugar
2 eggs, lightly beaten
1 tbsp milk
few drops of extract of rose oil
1/4 tsp vanilla essence
175 g/6 oz self-raising flour

frosting

6 tbsp butter, softened
175 g/6 oz icing sugar
pink or purple food colouring (optional)
silver dragées (cake decoration balls), to decorate

candied rose petals

12–24 rose petals
lightly beaten egg white, for brushing
caster sugar, for sprinkling

method

1 To make the candied rose petals, gently rinse the petals and dry well with kitchen paper. Using a pastry brush, paint both sides of a rose petal with egg white, then coat well with caster sugar. Place on a tray and repeat with the remaining petals. Cover the tray with foil and set aside to dry overnight.

2 Put 12 paper baking cases in a muffin pan, or place 12 double-layer paper cases on a baking sheet.

3 Put the butter and sugar in a bowl and beat together until light and fluffy. Gradually add the eggs, beating well after each addition. Stir in the milk, rose oil extract and vanilla essence then, using a metal spoon, fold in the flour. Spoon the mixture into the paper cases.

4 Bake the cupcakes in a preheated oven, 200°C/400°F, for 12–15 minutes or until well risen and golden brown. Transfer to a wire rack to cool.

5 To make the frosting, put the butter in a large bowl and beat until fluffy. Sift in the icing sugar and mix well together. If wished, add a few drops of pink or purple food colouring to complement the rose petals.

6 When the cupcakes are cold, spread a little frosting on top of each cake. Top with 1–2 candied rose petals and sprinkle with silver dragées to decorate.

christening cupcakes

ingredients

MAKES 24

400 g/14 oz butter, softened
400 g/14 oz caster sugar
finely grated rind of 2 lemons
8 eggs, lightly beaten
400 g/14 oz self-raising flour

topping

350 g/12 oz icing sugar
red or blue food colouring (liquid or paste)
24 sugared almonds

method

1 Put 24 paper muffin cases in a muffin pan.

2 Put the butter, sugar and lemon rind in a bowl and beat together until light and fluffy. Gradually add the eggs, beating well after each addition. Add the flour and, using a large metal spoon, fold into the mixture. Spoon the mixture into the paper cases to half-fill them.

3 Bake the cupcakes in a preheated oven, 180°C/350°F, for 20–25 minutes or until well risen, golden brown and firm to the touch. Transfer to a wire rack to cool.

4 When the cakes are cold, make the topping. Sift the icing sugar into a bowl. Add 6–8 teaspoons of hot water and stir until the mixture is smooth and thick enough to coat the back of a wooden spoon. Dip a skewer into the red or blue food colouring, then stir it into the icing until it is evenly coloured pale pink or pale blue.

5 Spoon a little icing on top of each cupcake. Top each with a sugared almond and allow to set for about 30 minutes before serving.

birthday party cupcakes

ingredients

MAKES 24

225 g/8 oz soft margarine
225 g/8 oz caster sugar
4 eggs
225 g/8 oz self-raising flour

topping

175 g/6 oz butter, softened
350 g/12 oz icing sugar
a variety of edible sugar flower shapes, cake decorating sprinkles, silver dragées (cake decoration balls), and sugar strands
various coloured tubes of writing frosting
24 birthday cake candles (optional)

method

1 Put 24 paper baking cases in a muffin pan, or place 24 double-layer paper cases on a baking sheet.

2 Put the margarine, sugar, eggs and flour in a large bowl and, using an electric hand whisk, beat together until just smooth. Spoon the mixture into the paper cases.

3 Bake the cupcakes in a preheated oven, 180ºC/350ºF, for 15–20 minutes or until well risen, golden brown and firm to the touch. Transfer to a wire rack to cool.

4 To make the frosting, put the butter in a bowl and beat until fluffy. Sift in the icing sugar and beat together until smooth and creamy. When the cupcakes are cold, spread a little frosting on top of each cupcake, then decorate to your choice and, if desired, place a candle in the top of each.

gold & silver anniversary cupcakes

ingredients

MAKES 24

225 g/8 oz butter, softened
225 g/8 oz caster sugar
1 tsp vanilla essence
4 large eggs, lightly beaten
225 g/8 oz self-raising flour
5 tbsp milk

topping

175 g/6 oz unsalted butter
350 g/12 oz icing sugar
silver or gold dragées (cake decoration balls)

method

1 Put 24 silver or gold foil cake cases in muffin pans, or arrange them on baking sheets.

2 Put the butter, sugar and vanilla essence in a bowl and beat together until light and fluffy. Gradually add the eggs, beating well after each addition. Add the flour and, using a large metal spoon, fold into the mixture with the milk. Spoon the mixture into the paper cases.

3 Bake the cupcakes in a preheated oven, 180°C/350°F, for 15–20 minutes or until well risen and firm to the touch. Transfer to a wire rack to cool.

4 To make the topping, put the butter in a large bowl and beat until fluffy. Sift in the icing sugar and beat together until well mixed. Put the topping in a piping bag fitted with a medium star-shaped tip.

5 When the cupcakes are cold, pipe icing on top of each. Sprinkle over the silver or gold dragées before serving.

feather-iced coffee cupcakes

ingredients

MAKES 16

1 tbsp instant coffee granules
1 tbsp boiling water
8 tbsp butter, softened, or soft margarine
115 g/4 oz brown sugar
2 eggs
115 g/4 oz self-raising flour
1/2 tsp baking powder
2 tbsp sour cream

icing

225 g/8 oz icing sugar
4 tsp warm water
1 tsp instant coffee granules
2 tsp boiling water

method

1 Put 16 paper baking cases in a muffin pan, or place 16 double-layer paper cases on a baking sheet.

2 Put the coffee granules in a cup or small bowl, add the boiling water and stir until dissolved. Set aside to cool slightly.

3 Put the butter, sugar and eggs in a bowl. Sift in the flour and baking powder, then beat the ingredients together until smooth. Add the dissolved coffee and the sour cream and beat together until well mixed. Spoon the mixture into the paper cases. Bake in a preheated oven, 190°C/375°F, for 20 minutes or until well risen and golden brown. Transfer to a wire rack to cool.

4 To make the icing, sift 140 g/5 oz of the icing sugar into a bowl, then gradually mix in the warm water to make a coating consistency that will cover the back of a wooden spoon. Dissolve the coffee granules in the boiling water. Sift the remaining icing sugar into a bowl, then stir in the dissolved coffee granules. Spoon the icing into a piping bag fitted with a fine nozzle. When the cupcakes are cold, coat the tops with the white icing, then quickly pipe the coffee icing in parallel lines on top. Using a skewer, draw it across the piped lines in both directions. Allow to set before serving.

lavender fairy cakes

ingredients

MAKES 12

115 g/4 oz golden caster sugar
115 g/4 oz butter, softened
2 eggs, beaten
1 tbsp milk
1 tsp finely chopped lavender flowers
$^{1}/_{2}$ tsp vanilla essence
175 g/6 oz self-raising flour, sifted
150 g/5$^{1}/_{2}$ oz icing sugar

to decorate

lavender flowers
silver dragées

method

1 Place 12 paper cake cases in a muffin pan. Place the caster sugar and butter in a bowl and cream together until pale and fluffy. Gradually beat in the eggs. Stir in the milk, lavender and vanilla essence, then carefully fold in the flour.

2 Divide the mixture between the paper cases and bake in a preheated oven, 200°C/400°F, for 12–15 minutes or until well risen and golden. The sponge should bounce back when pressed.

3 A few minutes before the cakes are ready, sift the icing sugar into a bowl and stir in enough water to make a thick icing.

4 When the fairy cakes are baked, transfer to a wire rack and place a blob of icing in the centre of each one, allowing it to run across the cake. Decorate with lavender flowers and silver dragées and serve as soon as the cakes are cool.

lemon butterfly cakes

ingredients

MAKES 12

115 g/4 oz self-raising flour
1/2 tsp baking powder
8 tbsp soft margarine
115 g/4 oz caster sugar
2 eggs, lightly beaten
finely grated rind of 1/2 lemon
2 tbsp milk
icing sugar, for dusting

lemon filling

6 tbsp butter, softened
175 g/6 oz icing sugar
1 tbsp lemon juice

method

1 Put 12 paper baking cases in a muffin pan, or place 12 double-layer paper cases on a baking sheet.

2 Sift the flour and baking powder into a large bowl. Add the margarine, sugar, eggs, lemon rind and milk and, using an electric hand whisk, beat together until smooth. Spoon the mixture into the paper cases.

3 Bake the cupcakes in a preheated oven, 190°C/375°F, for 15–20 minutes or until well risen and golden brown. Transfer to a wire rack to cool.

4 To make the filling, put the butter in a bowl and beat until fluffy. Sift in the icing sugar, add the lemon juice and beat together until smooth and creamy.

5 When the cupcakes are cold, use a serrated knife to cut a circle from the top of each cupcake and then cut each circle in half. Spread or pipe a little of the buttercream filling into the centre of each cupcake, then press the 2 semicircular halves into it at an angle, to resemble butterfly wings. Dust with a little sifted icing sugar before serving.

strawberry rose meringues

ingredients

MAKES 12

2 egg whites

115 g/4 oz caster sugar

filling

55 g/2 oz strawberries

2 tsp icing sugar

3 tbsp rose water

150 ml/5 fl oz double cream

to decorate

12 fresh strawberries

rose petals

method

1 Line 2 large baking sheets with non-stick baking parchment. Place the egg whites in a large, spotlessly clean, greasefree bowl and whisk until stiff peaks form. Whisk in half the sugar, then carefully fold in the remainder.

2 Spoon the meringue into a piping bag fitted with a large star nozzle. Make 24 x 7.5-cm/ 3-inch lengths onto the baking sheets. Bake in a preheated oven, 110°C/225°F, for 1 hour, or until the meringues are dry and crisp. Cool on wire racks.

3 To make the filling, place the strawberries in a blender or food processor and process to a purée. Strain the purée into a bowl and stir in the icing sugar and rose water. Place the cream in a separate bowl and whip until thick. Stir into the strawberry mixture and mix well together.

4 Fill the meringues with the strawberry cream. Cut 6 of the strawberries for the decoration in half and use to decorate the meringues. Scatter rose petals over the top and serve at once with the remaining whole strawberries.

zuccherini

ingredients

MAKES 12

175 g/6 oz plain chocolate, broken into pieces
10 Amaretti biscuits, crushed

mousse

55 g/2 oz plain chocolate, broken into pieces
1 tbsp cold, strong black coffee
2 eggs, separated
2 tsp orange-flavoured liqueur

to decorate

150 ml/5 fl oz double cream
2 tbsp cocoa powder
6 chocolate-coated coffee beans

method

1 To make the chocolate cups to hold the filling, put 175 g/6 oz plain chocolate in a heatproof bowl set over a saucepan of barely simmering water. Stir until melted and smooth, but not too runny, then remove the chocolate from the heat. Carefully coat the inside of 12 double paper cake cases with melted chocolate, using a small brush. Stand the chocolate cups on a plate and chill for at least 8 hours or overnight in the refrigerator.

2 To make the mousse, put the chocolate and coffee into a heatproof bowl set over a saucepan of barely simmering water. Stir over low heat until the chocolate has melted and the mixture is smooth, then remove from the heat. Cool slightly, then stir in the egg yolks and liqueur.

3 Whisk the egg whites in a separate bowl until stiff peaks form. Fold into the chocolate mixture with a metal spoon, then cool.

4 Remove the chocolate cups from the refrigerator and carefully peel off the paper cases. Divide the crushed Amaretti biscuits equally between the chocolate cups and top with the chocolate mousse. Return to the refrigerator for at least 30 minutes. Just before serving, whip the cream and pipe a star on the top of each chocolate cup. Dust half of the zuccherini with cocoa powder and decorate the other half with chocolate-coated coffee beans.

vanilla hearts

ingredients

MAKES 12

225 g/8 oz plain flour, plus extra for dusting
150 g/5½ oz butter, cut into small pieces, plus extra for greasing
125 g/4½ oz caster sugar, plus extra for dusting
1 tsp vanilla essence

method

1 Sift the flour into a large bowl. Add the butter and rub it in with your fingertips until the mixture resembles fine breadcrumbs. Stir in the caster sugar and vanilla essence and mix together to form a firm dough.

2 Roll out the dough on a lightly floured work surface to a thickness of 2.5 cm/1 inch. Stamp out 12 hearts with a heart-shaped biscuit cutter measuring 5 cm/2 inches across and 2.5 cm/1 inch deep. Arrange the hearts on a lightly greased baking sheet.

3 Bake in a preheated oven, 180°C/350°F, for 15–20 minutes or until the hearts are a light golden colour. Transfer the vanilla hearts to a wire rack to cool completely. Dust them with a little caster sugar just before serving.

gingerbread people

ingredients

MAKES 20, USING LARGE CUTTERS

450 g/1 lb plain flour, plus extra for dusting
2 tsp ground ginger
1 tsp allspice
2 tsp bicarbonate of soda
115 g/4 oz butter, plus extra for greasing
100 g/3½ oz golden syrup
115 g/4 oz brown sugar
1 egg, beaten

to decorate

currants
glacé cherries
85 g/3 oz icing sugar
3–4 tsp water

method

1 Sift the flour, ginger, allspice and bicarbonate of soda into a large bowl. Place the butter, syrup and sugar in a saucepan over low heat and stir until melted. Pour onto the dry ingredients and add the egg. Mix together to form a dough. The dough will be sticky to start with, but will become firmer as it cools.

2 On a lightly floured work surface, roll out the dough to about 3-mm/⅛-inch thick and stamp out gingerbread people shapes. Place on 3 large, greased baking sheets. Re-knead and re-roll the trimmings and cut out more shapes until the dough is used up. Decorate with currants for eyes and pieces of cherry for mouths. Bake in a preheated oven, 160°C/325°F, for 15–20 minutes or until firm and lightly browned.

3 Remove from the oven and cool on the baking sheets for a few minutes, then transfer to wire racks to cool completely. Mix the icing sugar with the water to a thick consistency. Place the icing in a small plastic bag and cut a tiny hole in one corner. Use the icing to draw buttons or clothes shapes on the cooled biscuits.

party biscuits

ingredients

MAKES 16

115 g/4 oz butter, softened, plus extra for greasing
115 g/4 oz brown sugar
1 tbsp golden syrup
1/2 tsp vanilla essence
175 g/6 oz self-raising flour
85 g/3 oz sugar-coated chocolate beans

method

1 Grease 2 baking sheets. Place the butter and sugar in a bowl and beat together with an electric whisk until light and fluffy, then beat in the syrup and vanilla essence.

2 Sift in half the flour and work it into the mixture. Stir in the chocolate beans and the remaining flour and work the dough together using a spatula.

3 Roll the dough into 16 balls and place them on the prepared baking sheets, spaced well apart to allow for spreading. Do not flatten them. Bake in a preheated oven, 180°C/350°F, for 10–12 minutes or until pale golden at the edges. Remove from the oven and cool on the baking sheets for 2 minutes, then transfer to wire racks to cool completely.

simply delicious

This chapter has recipes that are less indulgent, less showy, a little more simple and down-to-earth – but by no means boring!

Weekends are a great time for having a lazy 'brunch', that not-quite-breakfast, not-quite-lunch meal that goes hand in hand with reading your favourite magazine and catching up with the latest gossip with your family and friends. For a stylish brunch, make Doughnut Muffins, Lime and Poppy Seed Muffins and Simple Cinnamon Rolls. The aromas wafting from the oven will be marvellous, and while you are waiting for them to cool a little, you can make a stack of Apple Pancakes With Maple Syrup Butter.

For a simple but delicious accompaniment to your mid-morning cup of coffee, try Gingernuts – home-made are so much better than store-bought, a Drizzled Honey Cupcake, a fruity Rock Drop or a crumbly Eccles Cake. Almond Biscotti are absolutely perfect for dunking in a frothy cappuccino, and also make elegant petits fours to serve with after-dinner coffee.

On a cold winter's afternoon, serve Buttermilk Scones spread with whipped cream and strawberry jam, Sticky Gingerbread Cupcakes, warm, spicy Welsh Cakes, lemony Queen Cakes and buttery Petticoat Tail Shortbread. Very satisfying!

lime & poppy seed muffins

ingredients

MAKES 12

175 ml/6 fl oz sunflower or peanut oil, plus extra for oiling (if using)
225 g/8 oz plain flour
1 tsp baking powder
½ tsp salt
225 g/8 oz caster sugar
1 large egg
1 large egg white
150 ml/5 fl oz milk
1 tbsp lime juice
1 tbsp grated lime rind
2 tsp poppy seeds

to decorate

2 tsp grated lime rind
1–2 tsp poppy seeds

method

1 Oil a 12-cup muffin pan with sunflower oil, or line it with 12 muffin paper cases.

2 Sift the flour, baking powder and salt into a mixing bowl. Then add the caster sugar and stir together.

3 In a separate bowl, whisk the egg, egg white, remaining sunflower oil and milk together, then stir in the lime juice and grated lime rind. Add the egg mixture to the flour mixture, then add the poppy seeds and gently stir. Do not overstir the mixture – it is fine for it to be a little lumpy.

4 Divide the muffin mixture evenly between the 12 cups in the muffin pan or the paper cases (they should be about two-thirds full). Sprinkle over grated lime rind and poppy seeds to decorate, then bake in a preheated oven, 190°C/375°F, for 25 minutes or until risen and golden. Serve the muffins warm, or place them on a wire rack to cool.

doughnut muffins

ingredients

MAKES 12

175 g/6 oz butter, softened, plus extra for greasing
200 g/7 oz caster sugar
2 large eggs, lightly beaten
375 g/13 oz plain flour
3/4 tbsp baking powder
1/4 tsp bicarbonate of soda
pinch of salt
1/2 tsp freshly grated nutmeg
250 ml/9 fl oz milk

topping

100 g/3 1/2 oz caster sugar
1 tsp ground cinnamon
2 tbsp butter, melted

method

1 Grease a deep 12-cup muffin pan. In a large bowl, beat the butter and sugar together until light and creamy. Add the eggs, a little at a time, beating well between additions.

2 Sift the flour, baking powder, bicarbonate of soda, salt and nutmeg together. Add half to the creamed mixture with half of the milk. Gently fold the ingredients together before incorporating the remaining flour and milk. Spoon the mixture into the prepared muffin pan, filling each hole to about two-thirds full. Bake in a preheated oven, 180°C/350°F, for 15–20 minutes or until the muffins are lightly brown and firm to the touch.

3 For the topping, mix the sugar and cinnamon together. While the muffins are still warm from the oven, brush lightly with melted butter, and sprinkle over the cinnamon and sugar mixture. Eat warm or cold.

sticky gingerbread cupcakes

ingredients

MAKES 16

115 g/4 oz plain flour
2 tsp ground ginger
3/4 tsp ground cinnamon
1 piece of preserved ginger, finely chopped
3/4 tsp bicarbonate of soda
4 tbsp milk
6 tbsp butter, softened, or soft margarine
70 g/2 1/2 oz brown sugar
2 tbsp molasses
2 eggs, lightly beaten
pieces of preserved ginger, to decorate

frosting

6 tbsp butter, softened
175 g/6 oz icing sugar
2 tbsp ginger syrup from the preserved ginger jar

method

1 Put 16 paper baking cases in a muffin pan, or place 16 double-layer paper cases on a baking sheet.

2 Sift the flour, ground ginger and cinnamon together into a bowl. Add the finely chopped ginger and toss in the flour mixture until well coated. In a separate bowl, dissolve the bicarbonate of soda in the milk.

3 Put the butter and sugar in a bowl and beat together until fluffy. Beat in the molasses, then gradually add the eggs, beating well after each addition. Beat in the flour mixture, then gradually beat in the milk. Spoon the mixture into the paper cases.

4 Bake the cupcakes in a preheated oven, 160°C/325°F, for 20 minutes or until well risen and golden brown. Transfer to a wire rack to cool.

5 To make the frosting, put the butter in a bowl and beat until fluffy. Sift in the sugar, add the ginger syrup and beat together until smooth and creamy. Slice the preserved ginger into thin slivers or chop finely.

6 When the cupcakes are cold, spread a little frosting on top of each cupcake, then decorate with pieces of ginger.

drizzled honey cupcakes

ingredients

MAKES 12

85 g/3 oz self-raising flour
1/4 tsp ground cinnamon
pinch of ground cloves
pinch of grated nutmeg
6 tbsp butter, softened
85 g/3 oz caster sugar
1 tbsp honey
finely grated rind of 1 orange
2 eggs, lightly beaten
40 g/1 1/2 oz walnut pieces, finely chopped

topping

15 g/1/2 oz walnut pieces, finely chopped
1/4 tsp ground cinnamon
2 tbsp honey
juice of 1 orange

method

1 Put 12 paper baking cases in a muffin pan, or place 12 double-layer paper cases on a baking sheet.

2 Sift the flour, cinnamon, cloves and nutmeg together into a bowl. Put the butter and sugar in a separate bowl and beat together until light and fluffy. Beat in the honey and orange rind, then gradually add the eggs, beating well after each addition. Using a metal spoon, fold in the flour mixture. Stir in the walnuts, then spoon the mixture into the paper cases.

3 Bake the cupcakes in a preheated oven, 190°C/375°F, for 20 minutes or until well risen and golden brown. Transfer to a wire rack to cool.

4 To make the topping, mix together the walnuts and cinnamon. Put the honey and orange juice in a pan and heat gently, stirring, until combined.

5 When the cupcakes have almost cooled, prick the tops all over with a fork or skewer and then drizzle with the warm honey mixture. Sprinkle a little of the walnut mixture over the top of each cupcake and serve warm or cold.

marbled chocolate cupcakes

ingredients

MAKES 21

175 g/6 oz soft margarine

175 g/6 oz caster sugar

3 eggs

175 g/6 oz self-raising flour

2 tbsp milk

55 g/2 oz plain chocolate, melted

method

1 Put 21 paper baking cases in a muffin pan, or place 21 double-layer paper cases on a baking sheet.

2 Put the margarine, sugar, eggs, flour and milk in a large bowl and, using an electric hand whisk, beat together until just smooth.

3 Divide the mixture between 2 bowls. Add the melted chocolate to one bowl and stir together until well mixed. Using a teaspoon, and alternating the chocolate mixture with the plain mixture, put four half-teaspoons into each paper case.

4 Bake the cupcakes in a preheated oven, 180°C/350°F, for 20 minutes or until well risen and springy to the touch. Transfer to a wire rack to cool.

carrot cake

ingredients

MAKES 6

butter, for greasing
115 g/4 oz self-raising flour
pinch of salt
1 tsp ground allspice
1/2 tsp ground nutmeg
175 g/6 oz soft brown sugar
2 eggs, beaten
5 tbsp sunflower oil
175 g/6 oz grated carrots
1 banana, chopped
25 g/1 oz chopped toasted mixed nuts

frosting

3 tbsp butter, softened
3 tbsp cream cheese
175 g/6 oz icing sugar, sifted
1 tsp orange juice
grated rind of 1/2 orange
walnut halves or pieces, to decorate

method

1 Grease an 18-cm/7-inch square cake tin with butter and line with baking parchment. Sift the flour, salt, allspice and nutmeg into a bowl. Stir in the brown sugar, then stir in the eggs and oil. Add the carrots, banana and chopped mixed nuts and mix together well.

2 Spoon the mixture into the prepared cake tin and level the surface. Transfer to a preheated oven, 190°C/375°F, and bake for 55 minutes or until golden and just firm to the touch. Remove from the oven and cool. When cool enough to handle, turn out on to a wire rack to cool completely.

3 To make the frosting, put the butter, cream cheese, icing sugar, orange juice and orange rind into a bowl and beat together until creamy. Spread the frosting over the top of the cold cake, then use a fork to make shallow wavy lines in the frosting. Scatter over the walnuts, cut the cake into bars and serve.

simple cinnamon rolls

ingredients

MAKES 8 ROLLS

350 g/12 oz self-raising flour
pinch of salt
2 tbsp caster sugar
1 tsp ground cinnamon
100 g/3½ oz butter, melted, plus extra for greasing
2 egg yolks
200 ml/7 fl oz milk, plus extra for glazing

filling

1 tsp ground cinnamon
55 g/2 oz brown sugar
2 tbsp caster sugar
1 tbsp butter, melted

icing

125 g/4½ oz icing sugar, sifted
2 tbsp cream cheese, softened
1 tbsp butter, softened
about 2 tbsp boiling water
1 tsp vanilla essence

method

1 Grease a 20-cm/8-inch round tin and line the bottom with baking parchment.

2 Mix the flour, salt, caster sugar and cinnamon together in a bowl. Whisk the butter, egg yolks and milk together and combine with the dry ingredients to make a soft dough. Turn out onto a large piece of waxed paper, lightly sprinkled with flour, and roll out to a rectangle 30 x 25 cm/12 x 10 inches.

3 To make the filling, mix the ingredients together, spread evenly over the dough and roll up, Swiss-roll style, to form a log. Using a sharp knife, cut the dough into 8 even-sized slices and pack into the prepared tin. Brush gently with extra milk and bake in a preheated oven, 180°C/350°F, for 30–35 minutes or until golden brown. Remove from the oven and cool for 5 minutes before removing from the tin.

4 Sift the icing sugar into a large bowl and make a well in the centre. Place the cream cheese and butter in the centre, pour over the water and stir to mix. Add extra boiling water, a few drops at a time, until the frosting coats the back of a spoon. Stir in the vanilla essence, then drizzle the icing over the rolls. Serve warm or cold.

buttermilk scones

ingredients

MAKES 8

300 g/10½ oz self-raising flour, plus extra for dusting
1 tsp baking powder
pinch of salt
55 g/2 oz cold butter, cut into pieces, plus extra for greasing
40 g/1½ oz golden caster sugar
300 ml/10 fl oz buttermilk
2 tbsp milk
whipped cream, to serve
strawberry jam, to serve

method

1 Sift the flour, baking powder and salt into a bowl. Add the butter and rub in until the mixture resembles fine breadcrumbs. Add the sugar and buttermilk and quickly mix together.

2 Turn the mixture out onto a floured work surface and knead lightly. Roll out to 2.5-cm/1-inch thick. Using a 6-cm/2½-inch plain or fluted cutter, stamp out the scones and place on a greased baking sheet. Gather the trimmings, re-roll and stamp out more scones until all the dough is used up.

3 Brush the tops of the scones with milk. Bake in a preheated oven, 220°C/425°F, for 12–15 minutes or until well risen and golden. Transfer to a wire rack to cool. Split and serve with whipped cream and strawberry jam.

welsh cakes

ingredients

MAKES 16

225 g/8 oz self-raising flour
pinch of salt
55 g/2 oz white cooking fat
55 g/2 oz butter, plus extra for greasing
85 g/3 oz golden caster sugar
85 g/3 oz currants
1 egg, beaten
1 tbsp milk (optional)
caster sugar, for dusting

method

1 Sift the flour and salt into a bowl. Add the white cooking fat and butter and rub it in until the mixture resembles breadcrumbs. Stir in the sugar and currants. Add the egg and a little milk, if necessary, to make a soft, but not sticky, dough.

2 On a floured work surface, roll out the dough to 5 mm/1/4 inch thick. Stamp into circles with a 6-cm/2 1/2-inch plain or fluted cutter. Gather the trimmings, re-roll and stamp out more circles until all the dough is used up.

3 Grease a griddle or heavy-based frying pan and set over low heat. Cook the Welsh cakes for 3 minutes on each side, or until golden brown. Dust generously with caster sugar and serve warm or cold.

apple pancakes with maple syrup butter

ingredients

MAKES 18 PANCAKES TO SERVE 4–6

200 g/7 oz self-raising flour
100 g/3½ oz caster sugar
1 tsp ground cinnamon
1 egg
200 ml/7 fl oz milk
2 apples, peeled and grated
1 tsp butter

maple syrup butter

85 g/3 oz butter, softened
3 tbsp maple syrup

method

1 Mix the flour, sugar and cinnamon in a bowl and make a well in the centre. Beat the egg and the milk together and pour into the well. Using a wooden spoon, gently incorporate the dry ingredients into the liquid until well combined, then stir in the grated apple.

2 Heat the butter in a large, non-stick frying pan over low heat until melted and bubbling. Add tablespoons of the pancake mixture to form 9-cm/3½-inch circles. Cook each pancake for about 1 minute, until it starts to bubble lightly on the top and looks set, then flip it over and cook the other side for 30 seconds, or until cooked through. The pancakes should be golden brown; if not, increase the heat a little. Remove from the pan and keep warm. Repeat the process until all of the pancake mixture has been used up (it is not necessary to add extra butter).

3 To make the maple syrup butter, melt the butter with the maple syrup in a pan over low heat and stir until combined. To serve, place the pancakes on serving dishes and spoon over the flavoured butter. Serve warm.

queen cakes

ingredients

MAKES 18

8 tbsp butter, softened, or soft margarine
115 g/4 oz caster sugar
2 large eggs, lightly beaten
4 tsp lemon juice
175 g/6 oz self-raising flour
115 g/4 oz currants
2–4 tbsp milk, if necessary

method

1 Put 18 paper baking cases in a muffin pan, or place 18 double-layer paper cases on a baking sheet.

2 Put the butter and sugar in a bowl and beat together until light and fluffy. Gradually beat in the eggs, then beat in the lemon juice with 1 tablespoon of the flour. Using a metal spoon, fold in the remaining flour and the currants, adding a little milk if necessary, to give a soft dropping consistency. Spoon the mixture into the paper cases.

3 Bake the cupcakes in a preheated oven, 190°C/375°F, for 15–20 minutes or until well risen and golden brown. Transfer to a wire rack to cool.

rock drops

ingredients

MAKES 8

100 g/3½ oz butter, cut into small pieces, plus extra for greasing
200 g/7 oz plain flour
2 tsp baking powder
75 g/2¾ oz golden caster sugar
100 g/3½ oz sultanas
25 g/1 oz glacé cherries, finely chopped
1 egg, beaten
2 tbsp milk

method

1 Lightly grease a baking sheet, large enough for 8 big rock drops, with a little butter.

2 Sift the flour and baking powder into a mixing bowl. Rub in the butter with your fingertips until the mixture resembles fine breadcrumbs. Stir in the sugar, sultanas and chopped glacé cherries, mixing well. Add the beaten egg and the milk to the mixture and mix to form a soft dough.

3 Spoon 8 mounds of the mixture onto the prepared baking sheet, spacing them well apart as they will spread while cooking. Bake in a preheated oven, 200°C/400°F, for 15–20 minutes or until firm to the touch.

4 Remove the rock drops from the baking sheet. Either serve immediately or transfer to a wire rack to cool before serving.

eccles cakes

ingredients

MAKES 10–12

400 g/14 oz ready-made puff pastry
2 tbsp plain flour, for dusting
55 g/2 oz butter, softened
55 g/2 oz soft brown sugar
85 g/3 oz currants
25 g/1 oz mixed candied peel, chopped
½ tsp ground mixed spice (optional)
1 egg white, lightly beaten
1 tsp caster sugar

method

1 Roll out the pastry thinly, using the flour to dust the work surface and the rolling pin. Cut into rounds using a 9-cm/3½-inch cutter. Fold the trimmings carefully, re-roll and repeat the cuttings to give a total of 10–12 rounds.

2 In a bowl, mix together the butter and soft brown sugar until creamy, then add the dried fruit and mixed spice, if using.

3 Put a teaspoon of the filling in the centre of each pastry round. Draw the edges of the circles together and pinch the edges over the filling. Reshape each cake into a round. Turn the cakes over and lightly roll them with the rolling pin until the currants just show through. Score with a knife into a lattice pattern. Place on a greased baking sheet and set aside for 10–15 minutes.

4 Brush the cakes with the egg white, sprinkle with the caster sugar and bake at the top of a preheated oven, 220°C/425°F, for about 15 minutes until golden brown and crisp.

5 Transfer to a wire rack and sprinkle with a little more sugar if desired. Serve immediately, or store in an airtight tin for up to a week and reheat before serving.

orange & walnut cakes

ingredients

MAKES ABOUT 18

400 g/14 oz self-raising flour
1/2 tsp bicarbonate of soda
1/2 tsp ground cinnamon
1/4 tsp ground cloves
pinch of grated nutmeg
pinch of salt
300 ml/10 fl oz olive oil
75 g/2 3/4 oz caster sugar
finely grated rind and juice of 1 large orange

topping

25 g/1 oz walnut pieces, chopped finely
1/2 tsp ground cinnamon

syrup

175 g/6 oz Greek honey
125 ml/4 fl oz water
juice of 1 small lemon
juice of 1 small orange or 1 tbsp orange-flower water

method

1 Sift together the flour, bicarbonate of soda, cinnamon, cloves, nutmeg and salt.

2 Put the oil and sugar in a bowl and beat together. Add the orange rind and juice, then gradually beat in the flour mixture. Turn the mixture onto a lightly floured surface and knead for 2–3 minutes or until smooth.

3 Take small, egg-size pieces of dough and shape into ovals. Place on baking sheets, allowing room for spreading and, with the back of a fork, press the top of each cake twice to make a criss-cross design. Bake the cakes in a preheated oven, 180°C/350°F, for about 20 minutes or until lightly browned. Transfer to a wire rack to cool.

4 To make the topping, mix together the walnuts and cinnamon. To make the syrup, put the honey and water in a saucepan, bring to the boil, then simmer for 5 minutes. Remove from the heat and add the lemon juice and orange juice or orange-flower water.

5 When the cakes have almost cooled, use a slotted spoon to submerge each cake in the hot syrup and leave for about 1 minute. Place on a tray and top each with the walnut mixture. Cool completely before serving.

mincemeat crumble bars

ingredients

MAKES 12

400 g/14 oz ready-made mincemeat

icing sugar, for dusting

bottom layer

140 g/5 oz butter, plus extra for greasing

85 g/3 oz golden caster sugar

150 g/5$^1/_2$ oz plain flour

85 g/3 oz cornflour

topping

115 g/4 oz self-raising flour

6 tbsp butter, cut into pieces

85 g/3 oz golden caster sugar

25 g/1 oz flaked almonds

method

1 Grease a shallow 28 x 20-cm/11 x 8-inch cake tin. To make the bottom layer, beat the butter and sugar together in a bowl until light and fluffy. Sift in the flour and cornflour and, with your hands, bring the mixture together to form a ball. Push the dough into the cake tin, pressing it out and into the corners, then chill in the refrigerator for 20 minutes. Bake in a preheated oven, 200°C/400°F, for 12–15 minutes or until puffed and golden.

2 To make the crumble topping, place the flour, butter and sugar in a bowl and rub together into coarse crumbs. Stir in the flaked almonds.

3 Spread the mincemeat over the bottom layer and scatter the crumbs on top. Bake in the oven for a further 20 minutes or until golden brown. Cool slightly, then cut into 12 pieces and cool completely. Dust with sifted icing sugar, then serve.

petticoat tail shortbread

ingredients

MAKES 8 PIECES

175 g/6 oz plain flour, plus 1 tbsp for dusting

pinch of salt

55 g/2 oz caster sugar

115 g/4 oz butter, cut into small pieces, plus extra for greasing

2 tsp golden caster sugar

method

1 Mix together the flour, salt and sugar. Rub the butter into the dry ingredients. Continue to work the mixture until it forms a soft dough. Make sure you do not overwork the dough or the shortbread will be tough, not crumbly as it should be.

2 Lightly press the dough into a greased 20-cm/8-inch fluted cake tin. Alternatively, roll out the dough on a lightly floured work surface, place on a baking sheet and pinch the edges to form a scalloped pattern.

3 Mark into 8 pieces with a knife. Prick the shortbread all over with a fork and bake in the centre of a preheated oven, 150°C/300°F, for 45–50 minutes until the shortbread is firm and just coloured.

4 Cool in the tin and dredge with the sugar. Cut into portions and remove to a wire rack. Store in an airtight container in a cool place until needed.

almond biscotti

ingredients

MAKES 20–24

250 g/9 oz plain flour, plus extra for dusting

1 tsp baking powder

pinch of salt

150 g/5½ oz golden caster sugar

2 eggs, beaten

finely grated rind of 1 unwaxed orange

100 g/3½ oz whole blanched almonds, lightly toasted

method

1 Sift the flour, baking powder and salt into a bowl. Add the sugar, eggs and orange rind and mix to a dough, then knead in the almonds.

2 Using your hands, roll the dough into a ball, cut in half and roll each portion into a log about 4 cm/1½ inches in diameter. Place on a baking sheet lightly dusted with flour and bake in a preheated oven, 180°C/350°F, for 10 minutes. Remove from the oven and cool for 5 minutes.

3 Using a serrated knife, cut the logs into 1-cm/½-inch thick diagonal slices. Arrange the slices on the baking sheet and return to the oven for 15 minutes or until slightly golden. Transfer to a wire rack to cool and crisp up.

lavender biscuits

ingredients

MAKES 12

55 g/2 oz golden caster sugar, plus extra for dusting
1 tsp chopped lavender leaves
115 g/4 oz butter, softened, plus extra for greasing
finely grated rind of 1 lemon
175 g/6 oz plain flour

method

1 Place the sugar and lavender leaves in a food processor. Process until the lavender is very finely chopped, then add the butter and lemon rind and process until light and fluffy. Transfer to a large bowl. Sift in the flour and beat until the mixture forms a stiff dough.

2 Place the dough on a sheet of baking parchment and place another sheet on top. Gently press down with a rolling pin and roll out to 3–5-mm/1/8–1/4-inch thick. Remove the top sheet of paper and stamp out circles from the dough using a 7-cm/2 3/4-inch round biscuit cutter. Re-knead and re-roll the dough trimmings and stamp out more biscuits.

3 Using a spatula, carefully transfer the biscuits to a large, greased baking sheet. Prick the biscuits with a fork and bake in a preheated oven, 150°C/300°F, for 12 minutes or until pale golden brown. Cool on the baking sheet for 2 minutes, then transfer to a wire rack to cool completely.

gingernuts

ingredients

MAKES 30

350 g/12 oz self-raising flour
pinch of salt
200 g/7 oz caster sugar
1 tbsp ground ginger
1 tsp bicarbonate of soda
125 g/4½ oz butter,
plus extra for greasing
75 g/2¾ oz golden syrup
1 egg, beaten
1 tsp grated orange zest

method

1 Sift the self-raising flour, salt, sugar, ginger and bicarbonate of soda into a mixing bowl.

2 Melt the butter and golden syrup together in a saucepan over low heat. Remove the pan from the heat and cool the butter and syrup mixture slightly, then pour it onto the dry ingredients. Add the egg and orange zest and mix thoroughly to form a dough.

3 Using your hands, carefully shape the dough into 30 even-sized balls. Place the balls well apart on several baking sheets lightly greased with butter, then flatten them slightly with your fingers.

4 Bake in a preheated oven, 160°C/325°F, for 15–20 minutes or until golden. Carefully transfer the biscuits to a wire rack to cool.

orange cream cheese biscuits

ingredients

MAKES 30

225 g/8 oz butter, plus extra for greasing
200 g/7 oz brown sugar
85 g/3 oz cream cheese
1 egg, lightly beaten
350 g/12 oz plain flour
1 tsp bicarbonate of soda
1 tbsp fresh orange juice
1 tsp finely grated orange rind, plus extra for decorating
raw brown sugar, for sprinkling

method

1 Put the butter, sugar and cream cheese in a large bowl and beat until light and fluffy. Beat in the egg. Sift in the flour and bicarbonate of soda and add the orange juice and rind. Mix well.

2 Drop about 30 rounded tablespoonfuls of the mixture onto a large, greased baking sheet, making sure that they are well spaced apart. Sprinkle with the raw brown sugar.

3 Bake in a preheated oven, 190°C/375°F, for 10 minutes or until the biscuits are light golden brown at the edges.

4 Cool on a wire rack. Decorate with orange rind before serving.

healthy options

Leading a healthy lifestyle is sensible, desirable, and in some cases an absolute necessity – and it always seems to suggest an element of deprivation when it comes to those edible treats that add so much pleasure to life. If you have been diagnosed with diabetes or a heart problem, or have an intolerance to gluten or lactose, you will be pleased to know that you can still have the occasional cake.

If you are on a low-fat eating plan, the muffin recipes are ideal for you. Try Banana and Date Muffins, or Cranberry or Blueberry – and, to look at them, you won't believe that Spiced Wholemeal Muffins, Spiced Carrot Cake Muffins and Chocolate Brownies are also fine for you to eat! Diabetics can enjoy Honey and Lemon Muffins and Sugarless Chocolate Muffins – again, you'll be delighted to discover that these are a delicious option for you.

For a gluten or dairy intolerance, try Banana Muffins with Cinnamon Frosting and Chocolate Orange Mousse Cake – both these recipes use a gluten-free alternative to wheat and a dairy-free margarine.

If you simply want a healthy treat to keep you going through the day, try High-energy Muffins – the slow-release energy in oats will sustain you for hours!

banana muffins with cinnamon frosting

ingredients

MAKES 12

150 g/5½ oz gluten-free plain flour
1 tsp gluten-free baking powder
pinch of salt
150 g/5½ oz caster sugar
6 tbsp dairy-free milk
2 eggs, lightly beaten
150 g/5½ oz dairy-free margarine, melted
2 small bananas, mashed

frosting

50 g/1¾ oz vegan cream cheese
2 tbsp dairy-free margarine
¼ tsp ground cinnamon
90 g/3¼ oz icing sugar

method

1 Place 12 large paper cases in a deep muffin pan. Sift the flour, baking powder and salt together into a mixing bowl. Stir in the sugar.

2 Whisk the milk, eggs and margarine together in a separate bowl until combined. Slowly stir into the flour mixture without beating. Fold in the mashed bananas.

3 Spoon the mixture into the paper cases and bake in a preheated oven, 200°C/400°F, for 20 minutes or until risen and golden. Turn out onto a wire rack to cool.

4 To make the frosting, beat the cream cheese and margarine together in a bowl, then beat in the cinnamon and icing sugar until smooth and creamy. Chill the frosting in the refrigerator for about 15 minutes to firm up, then top each muffin with a spoonful.

banana & date muffins

ingredients

MAKES 12

vegetable oil cooking spray, for oiling (if using)
225 g/8 oz plain flour
2 tsp baking powder
1/4 tsp salt
1/2 tsp allspice
5 tbsp caster sugar
2 large egg whites
2 ripe bananas, sliced
55 g/2 oz no-soak dried dates, pitted and chopped
4 tbsp skimmed milk
5 tbsp maple syrup

method

1 Spray a 12-cup muffin pan with vegetable oil cooking spray, or line it with 12 muffin paper cases. Sift the flour, baking powder, salt and allspice into a mixing bowl. Add the caster sugar and mix together.

2 In a separate bowl, whisk the egg whites together. Mash the sliced bananas in a separate bowl, then add them to the egg whites. Add the dates, then pour in the milk and maple syrup and stir together gently to mix. Add the banana and date mixture to the flour mixture and then gently stir together until just combined. Do not overstir the mixture – it is fine for it to be a little lumpy.

3 Divide the muffin mixture evenly between the 12 cups in the muffin pan or the paper cases (they should be about two-thirds full). Bake in a preheated oven, 200°C/400°F, for 25 minutes or until risen and golden. Remove the muffins from the oven and serve warm, or place them on a wire rack to cool.

apple & raspberry muffins

ingredients

MAKES 12

- 3 large baking apples, peeled and cored
- 450 ml/16 fl oz water
- 1½ tsp allspice
- vegetable oil cooking spray, for oiling (if using)
- 300 g/10½ oz plain wholewheat flour
- 1 tbsp baking powder
- ¼ tsp salt
- 3 tbsp caster sugar
- 85 g/3 oz fresh raspberries

method

1 Thinly slice 2 baking apples and place them in a saucepan with 6 tablespoons of the water. Bring to the boil, then reduce the heat. Stir in ½ teaspoon of the allspice, cover the pan and simmer, stirring occasionally, for 15–20 minutes or until the water has been absorbed. Remove from the heat and cool. Blend in a food processor until smooth. Stir in the remaining water and mix well.

2 Spray a 12-cup muffin pan with vegetable oil cooking spray, or line it with 12 muffin paper cases. Sift the flour, baking powder, salt and remaining allspice into a mixing bowl. Then stir in the sugar.

3 Chop the remaining apple and add to the flour mixture. Add the raspberries, then combine gently with the flour mixture until lightly coated. Finally, gently stir in the cooled apple/water mixture. Do not overstir the mixture – it is fine for it to be a little lumpy.

4 Divide the muffin mixture evenly between the 12 cups in the muffin pan or the paper cases (they should be about two-thirds full). Bake in a preheated oven, 200°C/400°F, for 25 minutes or until risen and golden. Remove the muffins from the oven and serve warm, or place them on a wire rack to cool.

dairy-free berry muffins

ingredients

MAKES 12

- 1 large baking apple, peeled, cored and thinly sliced
- 3 tbsp water
- 1 tsp allspice
- 2 tbsp sunflower or peanut oil, plus extra for oiling (if using)
- 225 g/8 oz plain white or wholewheat flour
- 1 tbsp baking powder
- 1/4 tsp salt
- 40 g/1 1/2 oz wheat germ
- 25 g/1 oz fresh raspberries
- 25 g/1 oz fresh strawberries, hulled and chopped
- 6 tbsp maple syrup
- 175 ml/6 fl oz apple juice

method

1 Place the sliced apple and the water in a saucepan and bring to the boil. Reduce the heat and stir in half of the allspice, then cover the pan and simmer, stirring occasionally, for 15–20 minutes or until the water has been absorbed. Remove the pan from the heat and cool. Transfer the apple mixture to a food processor and blend until smooth.

2 Lightly oil a 12-cup muffin pan with a little sunflower oil, or line the pan with 12 muffin paper cases.

3 Sift the flour, baking powder, salt and the remaining allspice into a mixing bowl, then stir in the wheat germ.

4 In a separate bowl, mix the raspberries, strawberries, maple syrup, remaining oil, puréed apple and apple juice together. Add the fruit mixture to the flour mixture and gently stir until just combined. Do not overstir the mixture – it is fine for it to be a little lumpy.

5 Divide the muffin mixture evenly between the 12 cups in the muffin pan or the paper cases (they should be about two-thirds full). Transfer to a preheated oven, 190°C/375°F, and bake for 25 minutes or until risen and golden. Remove from the oven and serve warm, or place them on a wire rack to cool.

cranberry muffins

ingredients

MAKES 10

175 g/6 oz self-raising white flour
55 g/2 oz self-raising wholewheat flour
1 tsp ground cinnamon
1/2 tsp bicarbonate of soda
1 egg, beaten
70 g/2 1/2 oz thin-cut orange marmalade
150 ml/5 fl oz skimmed or semi-skimmed milk
5 tbsp corn oil
115 g/4 oz peeled, cored and finely diced eating apple
115 g/4 oz fresh or frozen cranberries, thawed if frozen
1 tbsp rolled oats
freshly squeezed orange juice, to serve

method

1 Line a muffin pan with 10 muffin paper cases.

2 Place the white and wholewheat flours, cinnamon and bicarbonate of soda in a mixing bowl and combine thoroughly.

3 Make a well in the centre of the flour mixture. In a separate bowl, blend the egg with the marmalade until well combined. Beat the milk and oil into the egg mixture, then pour into the dry ingredients, stirring lightly. Do not overmix – the mixture should be slightly lumpy. Quickly stir in the apple and cranberries.

4 Spoon the mixture evenly into the paper cases and sprinkle a little oats over each muffin. Bake in a preheated oven, 200°C/400°F, for 20–25 minutes or until well risen and golden, and a skewer inserted into the centre of a muffin comes out clean.

5 Lift out the muffins and transfer onto a wire rack. Cool for 5–10 minutes, then peel off the paper cases and serve warm with glasses of freshly squeezed orange juice. These muffins are best eaten on the day they are made – any leftover muffins should be stored in an airtight container and consumed within 24 hours.

blueberry muffins

ingredients

MAKES 12

vegetable oil cooking spray, for oiling (if using)
225 g/8 oz plain flour
1 tsp bicarbonate of soda
1/4 tsp salt
1 tsp allspice
115 g/4 oz caster sugar
3 large egg whites
3 tbsp low-fat margarine
150 ml/5 fl oz thick low-fat natural or blueberry-flavoured yogurt
1 tsp vanilla essence
85 g/3 oz fresh blueberries

method

1 Spray a 12-cup muffin pan with vegetable oil cooking spray, or line it with 12 muffin paper cases.

2 Sift the flour, bicarbonate of soda, salt and half of the allspice into a large mixing bowl. Add 6 tablespoons of the caster sugar and mix together.

3 In a separate bowl, whisk the egg whites together. Add the margarine, yogurt and vanilla essence and mix together well, then stir in the fresh blueberries until thoroughly mixed. Add the fruit mixture to the flour mixture, then gently stir until just combined. Do not overstir the mixture – it is fine for it to be a little lumpy.

4 Divide the muffin mixture evenly between the 12 cups in the muffin pan or the paper cases (they should be about two-thirds full). Mix the remaining sugar with the remaining allspice, then sprinkle the mixture over the muffins. Transfer to a preheated oven, 190°C/375°F, and bake for 25 minutes or until risen and golden. Remove the muffins from the oven and serve warm, or place them on a wire rack to cool.

fruity muffins

ingredients

MAKES 10

275 g/10 oz self-raising wholewheat flour
2 tsp baking powder
2 tbsp brown sugar
85 g/3 oz no-soak dried apricots, finely chopped
1 banana, mashed with 1 tbsp orange juice
1 tsp finely grated orange rind
300 ml/10 fl oz skimmed milk
1 large egg, beaten
3 tbsp sunflower or peanut oil
2 tbsp rolled oats
fruit spread, honey or maple syrup, to serve

method

1 Line 10 cups of a 12-cup muffin pan with muffin paper cases. Sift the flour and baking powder into a mixing bowl, adding any husks that remain in the sieve. Stir in the sugar and chopped apricots.

2 Make a well in the centre and add the mashed banana, orange rind, milk, beaten egg and oil. Mix together well to form a thick mixture and divide the mixture evenly between the muffin cases.

3 Sprinkle with a few rolled oats and bake in a preheated oven, 200°C/400°F, for 25–30 minutes until well risen and firm to the touch or until a toothpick inserted into the centre comes out clean.

4 Remove the muffins from the oven and place them on a wire rack to cool slightly. Serve the muffins while still warm with a little fruit spread, honey or maple syrup.

honey & lemon muffins

ingredients

MAKES 12

50 g/1¾ oz unrefined caster sugar
2 tbsp unsalted butter, melted and cooled slightly
150 ml/5 fl oz buttermilk
2 eggs, beaten
4 tbsp flower honey
finely grated rind of 1 lemon and juice of ½ lemon
225 g/8 oz plain flour
150 g/5½ oz oat bran
1½ tbsp baking powder

method

1 Line a 12-hole muffin pan with muffin paper cases. Put the sugar into a jug and add the butter, buttermilk, eggs, half the honey and lemon rind. Mix briefly to combine.

2 Sift the flour into a large mixing bowl, add the oat bran and baking powder, and stir to combine. Make a well in the centre of the flour mixture and add the buttermilk mixture. Quickly mix together – do not overmix; the mixture should be slightly lumpy.

3 Spoon the mixture into the paper cases and bake in a preheated oven, 180°C/350°F, for 25 minutes. Turn out onto a wire rack.

4 Mix the lemon juice with the remaining honey in a small bowl or jug and drizzle over the muffins while they are still hot. Let the muffins stand for 10 minutes before serving.

spiced carrot cake muffins

ingredients

MAKES 12

- 2 tbsp sunflower or peanut oil, plus extra for oiling (if using)
- 100 g/3½ oz plain white flour
- 100 g/3½ oz plain wholewheat flour
- 1 tsp bicarbonate of soda
- ¼ tsp salt
- 1 tsp ground cinnamon
- ½ tsp ground ginger
- 2 tbsp caster sugar
- 2 large egg whites
- 5 tbsp skimmed or semi-skimmed milk
- 225 g/8 oz canned pineapple chunks in juice, drained, chopped and mashed
- 250 g/9 oz carrots, grated
- 40 g/1½ oz sultanas
- 40 g/1½ oz shelled walnuts, chopped

topping

- 225 g/8 oz Quark (or any low-fat soft cheese)
- 1⅓ tbsp caster sugar
- 1½ tsp vanilla essence
- 1½ tsp ground cinnamon

method

1 Oil a 12-cup muffin pan with sunflower oil, or line it with 12 muffin paper cases. Sift both flours, bicarbonate of soda, salt, cinnamon and ginger into a mixing bowl. Add the caster sugar and mix together.

2 In a separate bowl, whisk the egg whites together, then mix in the milk and remaining oil. Add the mashed pineapple, the carrots, sultanas and walnuts and stir together gently. Add the fruit mixture to the flour mixture and stir gently until just combined. Do not overstir the mixture – it is fine for it to be a little lumpy.

3 Divide the muffin mixture evenly between the 12 cups in the muffin pan or the paper cases (they should be about two-thirds full). Transfer to a preheated oven, 190°C/375°F, and bake for 25 minutes or until risen and golden, then cool on a wire rack.

4 While the muffins are in the oven, make the topping. Place the Quark in a mixing bowl with the caster sugar, vanilla essence and 1 teaspoon of the cinnamon. Mix together well, then cover with clingfilm and transfer to the refrigerator until ready to use.

5 When the muffins have cooled to room temperature, remove the topping from the refrigerator and spread some evenly over the top of each muffin. Lightly sprinkle over the remaining cinnamon and serve.

potato & raisin muffins

ingredients

MAKES 12

- butter, for greasing and serving (optional)
- 175 g/6 oz floury potatoes, diced
- 125 g/4$^1/_2$ oz self-raising flour, plus extra for dusting
- 2 tbsp brown sugar
- 1 tsp baking powder
- 175 g/6 oz raisins
- 4 large eggs, separated

method

1 Lightly grease and flour a 12-cup muffin pan. Cook the diced potatoes in a saucepan of boiling water for 10 minutes or until tender. Drain well and mash until smooth. Transfer to a mixing bowl and add the flour, sugar, baking powder, raisins and egg yolks. Stir well to mix thoroughly.

2 In a clean, greasefree bowl, whisk the egg whites until they are standing in peaks. Using a metal spoon, gently fold them into the potato mixture until fully incorporated.

3 Divide the mixture evenly between the 12 cups in the muffin pan. Bake the muffins in a preheated oven, 200°C/400°F, for 10 minutes. Reduce the oven temperature to 160°C/325°F and bake the muffins for a further 7–10 minutes or until risen.

4 Remove the muffins from the oven and serve warm, buttered, if you like.

high-energy muffins

ingredients

MAKES 12

5 tbsp sunflower or peanut oil, plus extra for oiling (if using)
85 g/3 oz wholewheat flour
50 g/1¾ oz quick-cooking oats
40 g/1½ oz wheat germ
2 tsp baking powder
1 tsp ground cinnamon
¼ tsp salt
40 g/1½ oz no-soak dried dates, pitted and chopped
55 g/2 oz sultanas
115 g/4 oz bran flakes
200 ml/7 fl oz milk
2 large eggs, beaten
5 tbsp honey
4 tbsp golden syrup
4 tbsp molasses

method

1 Oil a 12-cup muffin pan with sunflower oil, or line it with 12 muffin paper cases. Place the flour, oats, wheat germ, baking powder, cinnamon and salt in a mixing bowl and mix together.

2 In a separate bowl, mix the dates, sultanas and bran flakes together. Pour in the milk and stir together, then stir in the beaten eggs, honey, golden syrup, molasses and remaining oil. Add the fruit mixture to the flour mixture and then gently stir until just combined. Do not overstir the mixture – it is fine for it to be a little lumpy.

3 Divide the muffin mixture evenly between the 12 cups in the muffin pan or the paper cases (they should be about two-thirds full). Transfer to a preheated oven, 190°C/375°F, and bake for 20–25 minutes or until risen and golden. Remove the muffins from the oven and serve warm, or place them on a wire rack to cool.

spiced wholewheat muffins

ingredients

SERVES 6

- 1 tbsp vegetable oil, plus extra for oiling
- 125 g/$4\frac{1}{2}$ oz plain flour
- $\frac{1}{2}$ tsp baking powder
- 55 g/2 oz wholewheat flour
- $\frac{1}{2}$ tsp ground allspice
- 1 egg, lightly beaten
- 150 ml/5 fl oz buttermilk
- 1 tsp grated orange zest
- 1 tbsp freshly squeezed orange juice
- 1 tsp low-sugar marmalade, for glazing

filling

- 100 g/$3\frac{1}{2}$ oz 0% fat Greek yogurt
- 1 tsp low-sugar marmalade
- $\frac{1}{2}$ tsp grated orange zest
- 100 g/$3\frac{1}{2}$ oz fresh raspberries

method

1 Oil a 6-hole muffin pan lightly with vegetable oil.

2 Sift the plain flour with the baking powder into a large mixing bowl. Using a fork, stir in the wholewheat flour and allspice until thoroughly mixed. Pour in the oil and rub into the flour mixture with your fingertips.

3 In a separate bowl, mix the egg, buttermilk and orange zest and juice together, then pour into the centre of the flour mixture and mix with a metal spoon, being careful not to overmix – the mixture should look a little uneven and lumpy.

4 Spoon the mixture into the prepared pan to come about three-quarters of the way up the sides of each hole. Bake in a preheated oven, 160°C/325°F, for 30 minutes or until golden brown and a skewer inserted into the centre of a muffin comes out clean. Remove from the oven and transfer to a wire rack. Brush with the marmalade and cool.

5 For the filling, mix the yogurt with the marmalade and orange zest. Cut the warm muffins through the centre and fill with the yogurt mixture and raspberries.

sugarless chocolate muffins

ingredients

MAKES 12

4 tbsp sunflower or peanut oil, plus extra for oiling (if using)
225 g/8 oz plain flour
1 tbsp baking powder
1 tbsp cocoa powder
$^1/_2$ tsp allspice
2 large eggs
175 ml/6 fl oz unsweetened orange juice
1 tsp grated orange rind
40 g/1$^1/_2$ oz fresh blueberries

method

1 Oil a 12-cup muffin pan with sunflower oil, or line it with 12 muffin paper cases. Sift the flour, baking powder, cocoa and allspice into a large mixing bowl.

2 In a separate bowl, whisk the eggs and the remaining sunflower oil together. Pour in the orange juice, add the grated orange rind and the blueberries, and stir together gently to mix. Add the egg and fruit mixture to the flour mixture and then gently stir together until just combined. Do not overstir the mixture – it is fine for it to be a little lumpy.

3 Divide the muffin mixture evenly between the 12 cups in the muffin pan or the paper cases (they should be about two-thirds full). Transfer to a preheated oven, 200°C/400°F, and bake for 20 minutes or until risen and golden. Serve the muffins warm, or place them on a wire rack to cool.

carrot bars

ingredients

MAKES 14–16

corn oil, for oiling
175 g/6 oz unsalted butter
85 g/3 oz brown sugar
2 eggs, beaten
55 g/2 oz self-raising wholewheat flour, sifted
1 tsp baking powder, sifted
1 tsp ground cinnamon, sifted
115 g/4 oz ground almonds
115 g/4 oz carrot, coarsely grated
85 g/3 oz sultanas
85 g/3 oz no-soak dried apricots, finely chopped
55 g/2 oz toasted chopped hazelnuts
1 tbsp flaked almonds

method

1 Lightly oil and line a shallow 25 x 20-cm/ 10 x 8-inch/ baking tin with non-stick baking parchment.

2 Cream the butter and sugar together in a mixing bowl until light and fluffy, then gradually beat in the eggs, adding a little flour after each addition.

3 Add all the remaining ingredients, except the flaked almonds. Spoon the mixture into the prepared tin and smooth the top. Sprinkle with the flaked almonds.

4 Bake in a preheated oven, 180°C/350°F, for 35–45 minutes or until the mixture is cooked and a skewer inserted into the centre comes out clean.

5 Remove from the oven and cool in the tin. Remove from the tin, discard the lining paper, and cut into bars.

fruit & nut squares

ingredients

MAKES 9

115 g/4 oz unsalted butter, plus extra for greasing
2 tbsp honey
1 egg, beaten
85 g/3 oz ground almonds
115 g/4 oz no-soak dried apricots, finely chopped
55 g/2 oz dried cherries
55 g/2 oz toasted chopped hazelnuts
25 g/1 oz sesame seeds
85 g/3 oz rolled oats

method

1 Lightly grease an 18-cm/7-inch shallow, square baking tin with butter. Beat the remaining butter with the honey in a bowl until creamy, then beat in the egg with the almonds.

2 Add the remaining ingredients and mix together. Press into the prepared tin, ensuring that the mixture is firmly packed. Smooth over the top.

3 Bake in a preheated oven, 180°C/350°F, for 20–25 minutes or until firm to the touch and golden brown.

4 Remove from the oven and allow to cool for 10 minutes before marking into squares. Cool completely before removing from the tin. Store in an airtight container.

super mocha brownies

ingredients

MAKES 12

150 g/5½ oz good-quality plain chocolate (70 per cent cocoa solids)
100 g/3½ oz dairy-free margarine, plus extra for greasing
1 tsp strong instant coffee
1 tsp vanilla essence
100 g/3½ oz ground almonds
175 g/6 oz caster sugar
4 eggs, separated
icing sugar, to decorate (optional)

method

1 Grease a 20-cm/8-inch square cake tin and line the bottom.

2 Melt the chocolate and margarine in a heatproof bowl placed over a saucepan of gently simmering water, making sure that the bottom of the bowl does not touch the water. Stir very occasionally until the chocolate and margarine have melted and are smooth.

3 Carefully remove the bowl from the heat. Cool slightly, then stir in the coffee and vanilla essence. Add the almonds and sugar and mix well until combined. Lightly beat the egg yolks in a separate bowl, then stir into the chocolate mixture.

4 Whisk the egg whites in a large bowl until they form stiff peaks. Gently fold a large spoonful of the egg whites into the chocolate mixture, then fold in the remainder until completely incorporated.

5 Spoon the mixture into the prepared tin and bake in a preheated oven, 180°C/350°F, for 35–40 minutes or until risen and firm on top but still slightly gooey in the centre. Cool in the tin, then turn out, remove the lining paper and cut into 12 pieces. Dust with icing sugar before serving, if liked.

chocolate brownies

ingredients

MAKES 12

butter, for greasing
55 g/2 oz unsweetened pitted dates, chopped
55 g/2 oz no-soak dried prunes, chopped
6 tbsp unsweetened apple juice
4 eggs, beaten
300 g/10½ oz brown sugar
1 tsp vanilla essence
4 tbsp low-fat drinking chocolate powder, plus extra for dusting
2 tbsp cocoa powder
175 g/6 oz plain flour
55 g/2 oz plain chocolate chips

icing

125 g/4½ oz icing sugar
1–2 tsp water
1 tsp vanilla essence

method

1 Grease and line an 18 x 28-cm/7 x 11-inch cake tin with baking parchment. Place the dates and prunes in a small saucepan and add the apple juice. Bring to the boil, cover and simmer for 10 minutes or until soft. Beat to form a smooth paste, then cool.

2 Place the cooled fruit in a mixing bowl and stir in the eggs, sugar and vanilla essence. Sift in the 4 tablespoons of drinking chocolate, cocoa and flour, and fold in along with the chocolate chips until well incorporated.

3 Spoon the mixture into the prepared tin and smooth over the top. Bake in a preheated oven, 180°C/350°F, for 25–30 minutes or until firm to the touch or until a skewer inserted into the centre comes out clean. Cut into 12 bars and cool in the tin for 10 minutes. Transfer to a wire rack to cool completely.

4 To make the icing, sift the sugar into a bowl and mix with enough water and the vanilla essence to form a soft, but not too runny, icing. Drizzle the icing over the chocolate brownies and leave to set. Dust with the extra chocolate powder before serving.

chocolate orange mousse cake

ingredients

SERVES 8

100 g/3½ oz caster sugar
100 g/3½ oz dairy-free margarine, plus extra for greasing
2 eggs, lightly beaten
100 g/3½ oz gluten-free plain flour
1 tsp gluten-free baking powder
2 tbsp cocoa powder
finely pared strips of orange rind, to decorate

mousse

200 g/7 oz good-quality plain chocolate (about 70 per cent cocoa solids)
grated rind of 2 oranges and juice of 1
4 eggs, separated

method

1 Cream the sugar and margarine together in a mixing bowl until pale and fluffy. Gradually add the eggs, beating well with a wooden spoon between each addition. Sift the flour, baking powder and cocoa powder together, fold half into the egg mixture, then fold in the remainder. Spoon the mixture into a greased and base-lined 23-cm/9-inch round, loose-based cake tin and level the surface with the back of a spoon. Bake in a preheated oven, 180°C/350°F, for 20 minutes or until risen and firm to the touch. Cool in the pan.

2 Meanwhile, melt the chocolate in a bowl placed over a saucepan of gently simmering water, making sure that the bottom of the bowl does not touch the water. Cool, then stir in the orange rind and juice and the egg yolks.

3 Whisk the egg whites in a large bowl until they form stiff peaks. Gently fold a large spoonful of the egg whites into the chocolate mixture, then fold in the remainder. Spoon the mixture on top of the cooked, cooled sponge and level the top with the back of a spoon. Place in the refrigerator to set. Remove the sides of the tin if not already removed (though not the bottom), then decorate with the orange rind strips and serve.